Fig.1: Music Week audience on Statehouse steps (ISHS)

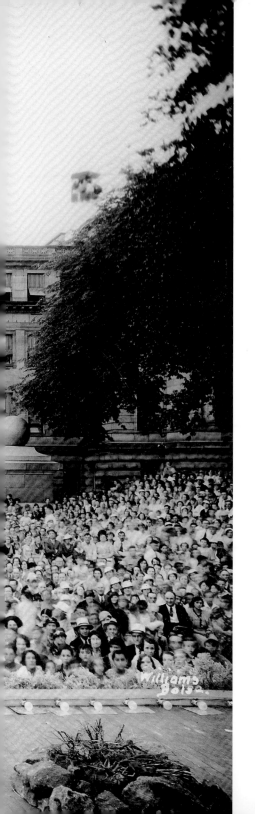

Boise Pops:

A Century of Music for the People of Boise

J. MEREDITH NEIL

SESQUICENTENNIAL EDITION DEDICATION
TERRI SCHORZMAN

FOREWORD
TOM TOMPKINS

55 PUBLICATIONS
BOISE, IDAHO

Photographs are used by permission of the Idaho State Historical Society, Idaho Statesman/Boise State University Albertson Library Archives, Boise School District, College of Idaho Robert Smylie Archives, and private collections. A complete listing of sources is on page x.

Cover Design: David Nels Reese, Moscow, Idaho
dnels@uidaho.edu; 208-310-6576

Editor/Production Manager: Diane Ronayne, Boise, Idaho
dianeronayne@gmail.com; 208-336-2128

Book Design: Chris Latter, Katy, Texas
chris.latter@gmail.com; 208-863-1889

Printed by Alexander Clark Printing, Boise, Idaho, in Boise, Idaho
UardaC@alexanderclark.com; 208-322-0611

ISBN 978-1-4675-7038-1

BOISE, IDAHO

P.O. Box 9133
Boise, ID 83707
55ProductionsBoise@gmail.com
208-333-8540
www.55Productions.org

Additional copies may be ordered from the address above, or look for "Boise Pops" at Boise bookstores, music venues or online at Amazon.com.

Boise High School Orchestra, c. 1939 (ISHS)

This book is dedicated to Byron Johnson, without whose inspiration and unflagging encouragement it would never have been written.

J.M. Neil

Fig. 2: Music Week Children's Orchestra, 1934 (ISHS)

Contents

Sesquicentennial Edition Dedication

When I attended McKinley Elementary in Boise in the 1960s, I was treated to an education in music that shaped my lifelong appreciation of this art form. Although I took private piano lessons for many years, my real understanding of the complexities and richness of music and its history came during those grade school years. I learned about an orchestra and the different types of instruments that comprise it. I learned how different the sounds from each instrument were and how remarkable they were when joined together. I was exposed to classical music traditions and the complexities and varieties of sounds. All the children sang in the choir and experienced the wonder of making music that brought our parents to tears. We learned the difference between alto and soprano and the ranges between voices…and so much more. Commitment to music education, as with all the arts, is essential in a child's development. It made a profound difference in my life.

As you read this book, you will see that my experience is not unique. For more than 100 years, literally thousands of Boise children and adults have been exposed to the benefits of music, thanks to the institutions, programs and people J.M. Neil describes in "Boise Pops." From the city's earliest days, when Boise was a regular stop for itinerant opera singers and internationally known concert musicians, popular music - "pops" - was performed for (and often by) the general citizenry, not just in the private homes of the wealthy.

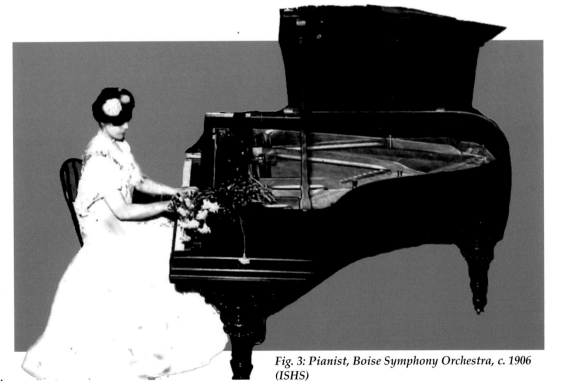

Fig. 3: Pianist, Boise Symphony Orchestra, c. 1906 (ISHS)

Since their founding, the city's public schools have offered music classes and performance opportunities to all students. A century later, the pioneers' instinctual support of music education was substantiated by scientific research identifying its valuable effects on learning. For example, playing a musical instrument has been shown to increase a child's ability to read and remember words and to process information; the size and structure of the brain itself is changed after as few as 15 months of practice.

The Boise School District and its patrons have consistently provided funds for music education, as well as support for the venerable, beloved institution of Music Week. First organized in 1918, Music Week now offers nine days of free organ recitals and band, dance and choral concerts, climaxed by a Broadway musical.

Performed by and for all ages, it's a truly community-wide celebration of music!

"The pops" also stimulate Boise's economy. Children who learn to appreciate music in school grow up to become ticket-buying audience members, volunteers and board members; some become professional musicians themselves. Performers take home paychecks; performance halls pay taxes and buy ads; audiences spend money on lodging, dining, shopping and other amenities. In our 2011 economic survey of Boise's nonprofit arts organizations, those devoted primarily to providing music (Boise Baroque Orchestra, Boise Music Week, Boise Philharmonic Association, Boise Rock School, Go Listen Boise and Opera Idaho) spent $2.577 million while serving 112,500 music lovers.

As Boiseans and visitors enjoy the many special events marking the city's 150th anniversary - our Sesquicentennial - in 2013, Mayor David Bieter and Boise's other elected leaders and staff hope they become aware of the factors that have combined to make today's community what it is. Universal access to live, popular music is surely one of them.

We trust that the citizens of today and tomorrow, like their forebears, will continue to value and invest in the myriad opportunities to enjoy popular music that truly set Boise apart as one of America's most livable cities. J.M. Neil has done us all a service by compiling this symphony of facts, faces and photographs to celebrate "Boise Pops."

Terri Schorzman
Director
Boise Department of Arts & History
March, 2013

Foreword

As I approach the 50th anniversary of my first performance with the Boise Philharmonic, I am struck by how many of the old guard have left us. The names and contributions of these trailblazing musicians, who conjure so many memories for me, are likely unknown to many of the newer arrivals to Idaho's music scene, yet today's artistic richness can be traced to the legacy these musical pioneers created. In an effort to keep their memory alive and appreciated, as chair of the orchestra committee in 2008 I asked the current Boise Philharmonic musicians to name all of their teachers who had themselves been members of the Boise Philharmonic. The resulting list was a veritable "Who's Who" of influential musicians, past and present, proving that we really do—and MUST—grow our own.

My family moved to Boise in 1962. The Treasure Valley presented to me a vibrant musical world where all the public schools enjoyed full orchestra, band and choir programs. Annual music festivals were sponsored by the school districts and Boise Tuesday Musicale. Music Week was enthusiastically supported by the community. Outstanding students competed for a chance to solo with the Boise Philharmonic, and the music teachers who performed with the Boise Philharmonic became our mentors, teachers, advisors, friends and colleagues. In the spirit of this book, I wish to acknowledge some of those who were most important to my development.

Lois Wuertz was principal viola. Over the years, she must have tutored hundreds, if not thousands, of students. I took weekly private lessons with her from 5th grade until I graduated from high school. She had many insights into the technical aspects of approaching the viola because, as an adult, she was forced to relearn the instrument following a terrible car accident. Going well beyond sharing those important technical suggestions, she brought to our lessons her deep love of music. By 1968, I was sitting with her in the Boise Philharmonic, which gave me a front row seat to her leadership skills.

Jim Hopper was principal clarinet. He was also my orchestra teacher for three years at West Junior High. A Juilliard graduate, he encouraged stylistic experimentation and exploration with his sense of humor and infectiously playful approach to music.

Jim Perkins was principal horn, as well as my orchestra teacher at Borah High. He may have seen my inclination toward a career in music before I did. To illustrate: As a junior, I asked if I could play violin in the orchestra that year. He thoughtfully considered and then said, "Yes… IF you'll play drums for me in marching band." As a senior, I asked if I could play cello. He replied, "Yes… IF you'll continue with the drums AND play string bass for me in symphonic band!" In other words, I asked to work hard and he said, "Work harder still!" What wonderful opportunities he presented me. I'm so grateful.

I also took lessons from other Boise Philharmonic musicians, including viola from Kathryn Mitchell (violin), conducting from Mel Shelton (trumpet), and theory with Wally Bratt (cello).

Henry von der Heide was one of the conductors for the Boise Civic

Symphony (the predecessor to the Boise Philharmonic). However, I knew him best from playing under his direction during the lavish half-time shows he produced for the Boise vs. Borah Veteran's Day rivalry football game!

My memory is that violinists Stella Margaret Hopper, Walter Cervany, Leona Underkoffler, Leah Telford and June Itami all sat as concertmaster at one time or another and touched an entire generation. The cello section was filled with students of Catherine Bieler, and John Best taught bass.

In 1962, the Boise Philharmonic had just incorporated into its current form, with Jacques Brourman as the conductor. He had the reputation for being a taskmaster. Rumor had it that he'd stop in the middle of the rehearsal, point to the rookie and say, "Play that [difficult] passage!" My first concert with the Boise Philharmonic was in 1966, when I was a 9th grader. The maestro must have taken pity on me, for he refrained from putting me under that microscope, and I am eternally thankful!

Mathys Abas stepped onto the conductor's podium in 1967. He had been in the Dutch Resistance during the Second World War and brought a broader worldview to our provincial little town.

I remember the first time we tackled the challenging "Concerto for Orchestra" by Bartok—or did IT tackle US?

Dan Stern continued to improve our sound, but was also instrumental in turning the Boise Philharmonic into a suc-

Fig. 4: Tom Tompkins (flute), Blue Jays U.K. Tour, 1976. (Tompkins)

cessful business. He was responsible for creating the salaried positions held by the principal players who comprise the Woodwind Quintet, the Brass Quintet and the String Quartet. Jim Ogle had the longest tenure—20 years—and concentrated upon improving the "precision" of our sound. Robert Franz, our current conductor, brings us an abundance of joy, enthusiasm and vision.

Throughout all these changes, I have been impressed by the overwhelming support of the community, support that embraces more than just classical music. I remember the farmers I met at the Grange

Halls for fun-filled evenings of fiddle and bluegrass music and the patients in nursing homes whose eyes lit up when we'd play their old-time favorites. There were the crowds that gathered for the Boise State University Summerfest Concerts and Boise Philharmonic Pops in the Park, and those who came to listen to my first folk/rock group, Providence, witnessing my baby steps into the world of improvisation. I am grateful for the dedicated followers who have tracked my career from its early days in Boise to rock-and-roll in England, orchestras in Mexico and touring throughout Europe, then to my return to Boise as principal viola and my jazz collaborations with Kevin Kirk and Onomatopoeia. Musicians appreciate and need this kind of vital interaction with our listeners!

Thanks to Boise's rich musical history and its citizens' interest and involvement in the arts, music is thriving all around us. I feel honored and fortunate to have been a part of it, and I applaud J.M. Neil for keeping our musical heritage alive and in focus by writing this book.

Tom Tompkins

Tom Tompkins
Manager, Esther Simplot Performing Arts Academy
Boise, 2013

Photography Credits

Private Collections: Helen Bivens (Fig. 57); Burt Burda (Fig. 63), Mary and C. Griffith Bratt (Figs. 24, 69, 97), Bill Jamison (Figs. 59, 64), Byron Johnson (Figs. 47, 48), Steve Fulton (Fig. 121), J.M. Neil (Figs. 62, 76, 79, 134), Carolyn Panko (Figs. 80, 130), Diane Ronayne (Fig. 84), June Schmitz (Fig. 73, 126, 132), Tom Tompkins (Figs. 4, 92, 93, 118), Laura von der Heide (Figs. 65, 66, 81), Boise Philharmonic (Fig. 78).

Boise Dept. of Parks & Recreation: Fig. 13

Boise State University, Albertsons Library Archive: Fig. 61
        MSS 111, Idaho Statesman Photo Collection: Figs. 60, 77, 83, 90, 91, 94-96, 98-100, 102-105, 107-116, 120

The College of Idaho, Caldwell, Idaho
        Robert E. Smylie Archives, Beale Collection: Figs. 14,15, 18, 35, 39-41
        Freddie Loucks: Fig. 124

Idaho State Historical Society:
        Browsing collection: Figs. 2 (2987); 5,7 (65-132.3,4); 6 (72-3.15); 8 (72-28.13); 9 (72-39.8); 10 (73-98.23); 11 (1087); 12 (62-168.3); 16 (64-37.29); 17 (68-74.6); 29 (So 62-20.12853); 30 (78-5.63H); 31 (Si 62-208570); 37 (82-59.6); 44 (82-597.D); copyright page (2985); inside back cover Fig. 114 (2986).
        Yearbook collection, Boise High School "Courier" (Boise School District): Figs. 22, 36, 46, 51
        Ar series 200620/#10041: Fig. 58
        MS 50: Box 1: Figs. 23, 25, 34, 71, 72, 74; Box 2 - Figs. 55, 56; Box 4, file 3 - Fig. 67; Scrapbook 1 - Fig. 28
        MS301: Box 1: Fig. 75; Box 4 - Figs. 26, 68, 70
        MS356, Box 5: Fig. 20
        MS511: Box 1: Fig. 45; Box 3 - Figs. 27, 32 (794), 50 (943)
        MS544: Box 4, Pam 13: Fig. 33

Internet
        Figs. 19, 21, 38, 42, 43, 49, 52-54, 82, 85, 88, 89, 106, 117, 119, 123, 125, 128, 129, 131, 133, 135, 136
        Figs. 86, 87: pnwbands.com
        Fig. 122: matusiak.org
        Fig. 127: farm4.static.flickr.com

Acknowledgements

In a project of this magnitude, many individuals contributed to the final publication. Dan Stern, John Stedman, Tony Boatman and Tom Tompkins gave early encouragement and endorsement. Philanthropist Esther Simplot, numerous members of the Boise High School Class of '55 and other generous souls stepped forward with funds to underwrite publication costs; some are graciously volunteering to sell the book during Boise's Sesquicentennial Commemoration, Boise 150.

Special thanks is due to those who generously loaned images from their private collections, to the Idaho Statesman for granting permission to reprint photographs without charge, and to archivists Alan Virta, Julia Stringfellow, Jim Duran and their staff (BSU Library Special Collections), Jan Boles (College of Idaho archive), and Jenaleigh Kiebert, Steve Barrett, their staff and volunteers Dave Crawforth and Max Burke (Idaho State Historical Society Archive). Their patient labors provided the 140 images you see in this book.

Cover artist D. Nels Rees and book designer Chris Latter melded scores of disparate elements into an elegant whole. Alan Virta masterfully compiled the index. Mark Baltes and Terri Schorzman invited our participation in Boise 150 events and the Boise 150 SesquiShop. Kay Hardy and Gregory Kaslo offered display space at their Egyptian Theater.

My fellow members of the board of directors of 55 Productions (Jeanne Belfy, Wally Pond, D. Nels Reese, Dwayne Rife, John Runft, Julia Stringfellow, Ron Thurber and Alan Virta) provided the publishing structure as well as continuous support, personally and professionally. The board joins me in thanking and acknowledging Diane Ronayne for her efforts in pulling together all these components and more to bring this book to completion.

I am delighted that proceeds from book sales will assist students pursuing musical studies and local artists, through grants from 55 Productions, an Idaho nonprofit organization.

J. M. Neil, Boise
April 2, 2013

Fig. 5: Drummer, Columbia Band, 1910 (ISHS).

Free Music on Main Street

IT ALL STARTED WITH THE COLUMBIA BAND IN 1910

For more than a century, the tradition of free music performed in an open-

air setting for public enjoyment has been alive and well in Boise. It echoes

in the Alive After Five concerts in The Grove Plaza and events like the Boise

Musical Festival held at Ann Morrison Park. Its roots can be traced to a

crisp October morning in 1910.

On Oct. 11, 1910, the Columbia Band entertained music lovers in downtown Boise with a free, outdoor concert. It was during the week when the Idaho Intermountain Fair was being held a few miles away. The band's performances, which continued each day of the fair, began at 10 a.m. at the corner of 9th and Main streets, where the Wells Fargo Bank building stands in 2013. These concerts heralded a new era for musical expression in Boise.

They were not the first in the history of this little frontier city to be offered to the public without charge. However, never before had the local newspaper, the *Idaho Statesman*, seen fit to publish an entire concert program—more than 50 selections played over the course of the week.

More importantly, the relaxed, festive style of the Columbia Band's fair week performances contrasted greatly with the style and emotional ambience previously prevalent in Boise musical performances. This difference is reflected in the posture assumed by the band for its portrait (*figure* 7), a far cry from the stiff formality prescribed by Victorian social leaders of an earlier day.

The old order was typified by gatherings such as the one reported by the *Statesman* in September 1910. The paper noted that on a Friday afternoon,

Fig. 6: Sherman House (ISHS)

a small group of ladies gathered at the Harrison Boulevard home of Mrs. Harry Wyman to hear a variety of musical selections. What counted was not so much what was performed or how well, but who was doing it. The newspaper report carefully listed the names and marital status of all of the performers, but failed to indicate whether they sang or played an instrument.

MUSIC FOR THE PUBLIC AT LARGE

Such gatherings reflected an attitude embodied in the stolid exterior of Sherman House (*figure* 6), a genteel boarding house across Jefferson Street from the State Capitol. It opened in 1890, operated by the sister of Mary Hallock Foote. Mrs. Foote was a noted writer and artist from New York whose engineer husband had taken a job designing an irrigation canal system proposed for the Boise River Valley. Sherman House was a fashionable venue for elite musical gatherings. Some who attended them, however, voiced disdain for the common local scene and the people busy building Boise into something greater than a frontier town.

"There is something terribly sobering about these solitudes, these waste places," Mrs. Foote lamented. "They belittle everything one is, or tries to do."

The Footes soon moved elsewhere, but this attitude lingered on among

Fig. 7: Columbia Band, 1910 (ISHS)

Boise's social elite until the Columbia Band's fair week concert series ushered in a whole new stance, much more optimistic and confidently determined to provide music for the public at large.

Prior to 1910, public musical performances in Boise were limited in frequency as well as in variety. Minstrel shows, both by traveling companies and those produced by local talent, regularly drew sizable audiences. Performances by the regimental band stationed at Boise Barracks always received appreciative attention. The occasional piano or

vocal recital gained an approving nod. However, as the *Statesman* conceded in 1899 after noting the poor attendance at one concert: "Boise is not musical, that is not in the classical sense. That has often been demonstrated." Except for opera, which is discussed in Chapter 3, this remained generally true for the next decade.

The backwardness of Boise's concert life during this era might be attributed to the lack of attractive performance spaces. Peter Sonna's Opera House (*figure* 8) dated back to territorial days

and certainly showed its age. Until James Pinney replaced his antiquated Columbia Theater (*figure* 10) with the Pinney Theater in 1908 (*figure* 9), Boise did not have a performance space it could offer with pride to visiting performers. Even the Pinney did not dramatically enhance the quality of concerts during its first years. However, some performers, like Ignacy Paderewski, the world-renowned Polish pianist, did find the earlier facilities adequate. Paderewski played to a packed house at the Columbia on Feb. 10, 1908, seven months before the Pinney opened.

Nor can one point convincingly to Boise's small population and limited means to explain the lack of concerts prior to 1910. Numerous traveling opera companies found sufficient patronage to perform for several days or even a week in Boise. Also, local pocketbooks easily met Paderewski's fee of $2,500, even though tickets did not go on sale until five days before the concert.

The most important constraint on public performances prior to the Columbia Band's fair week series was the genteel aloofness embodied in Mary Hallock Foote's negative

Fig. 8: Sonna Opera House, interior, c. 1900. (ISHS)

Fig. 9: Pinney Theater, interior, 1908. (ISHS)

Fig. 10: Columbia Theater, c. 1890s. (ISHS)

critique. The "best people" — those who might be found at a Sherman House soiree—firmly believed that music should be edifying, that music lovers should be properly informed about the cultural context of the music they were hearing, and that dignity should be resolutely maintained during all performances. Such criteria indicated little concern for the tastes or the enjoyment of the average person. A striking example of this attitude may be found in the brief history of the Philharmonic Musical Society.

PHILHARMONIC MUSICAL SOCIETY

Organized in 1901 by a group of socially prominent ladies to present classical music concerts by local performers as well as visiting talent, the Society managed to stage an ambitious choral festival in 1903. In October 1904, it reorganized to gain a "more substantial footing." Those wishing to attend the concerts and lectures would pay dearly for the privilege: an annual membership fee of $3 as well as an assessment of $.25 each month. The Society asserted: "[T]he tuition and practice which the members will obtain should compensate many times for the cost...." Evidently, few people agreed; nothing more was heard of this Society.

BOISE SYMPHONY ORCHESTRA

Local orchestral musicians hoped for better results. Thirty of them gathered at the Boston Grill for a banquet in January 1906. "A great deal of enthusiasm was displayed," according to the *Statesman*, and those attending proceeded to organize the Boise Symphony Orchestra with Mose Christensen as the conductor. It had a very promising start, with numerous published letters of support. The

Fig. 11: Boise Symphony Orchestra on stage, 1906. (ISHS)

following spring to finish paying all of the musicians. Little wonder that Christensen left later that year for greener pastures in Portland. The Boise Symphony Orchestra lingered on for a decade, offering a concert every year or two, but vanished after 1916. It would be another 50 years before Boise found the formula for a sustainable community orchestra.

BOISE MUNICIPAL BAND

It turned out to be far easier to establish the Boise Municipal Band. In April 1912, Columbia Band director C. M. Daggett approached the Commercial Club, the predecessor of the Chamber of Commerce, asking for its cooperation in "organizing a first-class concert band in Boise." He stressed that the musicians needed regular payment for their services. The Commercial Club board responded favorably, and Mayor Arthur Hodges assured them of his support. The City Council, however, initially rebuffed the whole idea of using city funds for music. In September, it denied the request for $40 for a band to greet visitors from the national capital. Council

musicians cut a handsome figure on stage (*figure* 11) and received an appreciative response from the full house attending their first concert, held at the Columbia Theater on April 17, 1906.

Later that year, the National Irrigation Congress gathering in Boise on Sept. 5 gave the orchestra the chance to entertain an audience drawn from all parts of the nation. That performance, heard by thousands at Riverside Park, went off without a hitch — except for one pesky detail. Since no admission was charged, costs totaling $562.55 had to be met by contributions. Despite the assistance of several community leaders, including Episcopal Bishop James Funsten, the orchestra was still struggling the members doubted they had any legal basis for making such an appropriation.

Three years later, a committee of Columbia Band members gained a far friendlier response from the council. In a lengthy statement published in full by the *Statesman*, the committee reported that it had consulted with other cities regarding the costs of a municipal band and found it amounted to $5,000 annually. Typical of Boiseans' attitudes, then and since, no one quarreled with the assumption that Boise (with a population of only 17,358, according to the 1910 census) should model its policies after much larger cities such as Portland, Seattle, Kansas City and Fort Worth. While the council did not spring for the full $5,000, on Aug. 6, 1915, it did approve $1,000 for the remainder of the season. This provided $2.50 per performance for each musician, which was a fair wage for a working man.

The director received $4 per performance, also a tolerable rate for the times. The original $1,000 did not include the cost of uniforms, but the Boise Municipal Band soon received handsome outfits (*figure* 12).

The musicians wasted no time merging the Columbia Band into the Municipal Band, offering its first concert on Sept. 26, 1915. Typical of many later performances, it was played from the Capitol steps. (The band shell in Julia Davis Park, *figure* 13, where more recent free concerts have been staged, was not constructed until 1928.)

The public loved the band's performance. An "enormous crowd" warmly applauded the "splendid concert," according to the *Statesman*. The band played—as it continued to do throughout the 70 years of its

Fig. 13: Band shell, Julia Davis Park (BP&R)

Fig. 12: Municipal Band, c. 1915 (ISHS)

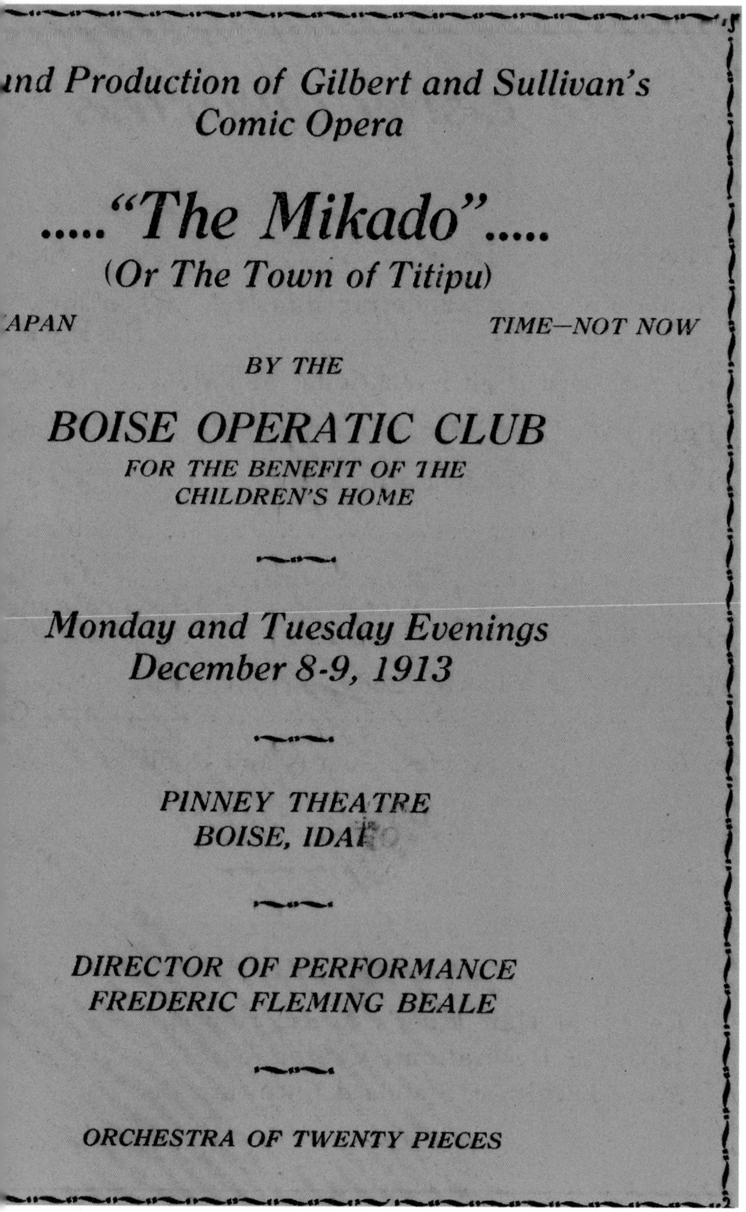

ınd Production of Gilbert and Sullivan's Comic Opera

....."The Mikado".....
(Or The Town of Titipu)

APAN   TIME—NOT NOW

BY THE

BOISE OPERATIC CLUB
FOR THE BENEFIT OF THE CHILDREN'S HOME

Monday and Tuesday Evenings
December 8-9, 1913

PINNEY THEATRE
BOISE, IDAH

DIRECTOR OF PERFORMANCE
FREDERIC FLEMING BEALE

ORCHESTRA OF TWENTY PIECES

Figure 14: Program cover, "The Mikado" 1913 (CofI)

existence a program of short, lively selections aimed to please a broad audience, offering occasions for toe-tapping rather than pensive contemplation.

The Municipal Band performed frequently, commonly once a week during the summer months, and occasionally it also provided something special. Culminating the July 4th celebration in 1917, for example, it invited the public to a street dance on Jefferson Street, blocked off between 6th and 8th streets. The band played for dancing until midnight, at the foot of the Capitol steps. Some in the large crowd came only to watch and listen. Others donned costumes to enhance their enjoyment of this free, open-air ball— the first of its kind in Boise—that set a precedent frequently followed in subsequent years.

BEALE, WESBROOK AND FARNER

Obviously, Boise's musical life went through major changes during the few short years following the Columbia Band's fair week series. Those changes derived in no small measure from the arrival of three men: two Midwesterners in 1911—Frederic Fleming Beale and Arthur Wesbrook—and Eugene Farner from New York in 1912. All three demonstrated notable musical talent as well as outstanding organizational abilities; the combined impact of their efforts dramatically changed the character of Boise's concert life.

Fig. 15: Frederic Fleming Beale (CofI)

Beale (*figure* 15), the eldest and most experienced of the three, settled in Caldwell, where his wife had family. He had spent the previous four years in Seattle as head of the University of Washington piano department and organist at the First Methodist Church. He set up the Beale School of Music, which functioned as the music program at the College of Idaho until 1925, when it formally merged with the College. Beale also became organist for Caldwell's new Methodist church, which reputedly had the finest pipe organ in the state.

Beale, however, sought much more

Fig. 16: Boise High School Chorus, c. 1910 (ISHS)

than Caldwell had to offer. After organizing a short-lived choral society there, he began commuting to Boise for larger challenges, a practice he continued until his retirement in 1947. His first two ventures came to naught: the Fellowship Singers, a male chorus that performed

twice in 1913 but then disappeared, and the Boise Operatic Company, which produced Gilbert & Sullivan's "The Mikado" in December 1913 (*figure* 14) and thereafter vanished. Nevertheless,

Beale quickly found a warm reception with music-minded Boiseans, which eventually led in the 1920s to a very well-paid position as organist at St. John's Cathedral but could have been predicted by the close of 1913. The January 1914 performance of Handel's "Messiah"

included a prominent role for Beale as pianist.

Arthur Wesbrook, who directed that performance of "Messiah," spent barely three years in Boise. Nonetheless, his influence on the city's musical development was significant. There was no report in the *Statesman* of his arrival as musical director for Boise High School. By the spring of 1913, however, the newspaper referred to him as an "accomplished young musical director," and in its review of "Messiah" left no doubt that Wesbrook had a great deal to do with the "musical progress made in Boise in the past three years," which it saw as "little short of marvelous."

MUSIC IN THE SCHOOLS

Wesbrook was not the first music teacher at Boise High School, but its musical curriculum had barely been set in place by the time he arrived (*figure* 16). The very first glee club originated in December 1903, when 10 or 12 girls were gathered to provide music for school occasions. The orchestra began the following year, but the band did not appear until 1909, when the principal,

C.F. Rose, acted as conductor. The school's performance record did include a few highlights. In December 1907, for example, a chorus composed of 250 men and women presented a concert.

Nevertheless, music in the schools remained irregular. The orchestra, as seen in a photograph published in 1911, included 13 strings and 14 wind instruments—far from a conventional orchestral instrumentation. Wesbrook soon set a much higher performance level, which remained a permanent

characteristic of public school concerts. It could already be seen in the 1913 production of an operetta, "Rose Marden." Accompanied by an orchestra of 40, the 250-voice chorus was, a reviewer declared, "without doubt one of the best heard in the city in some time."

BOISE CHORAL SOCIETY

Wesbrook had an even greater effect on the community music

scene. Prior to 1911, Boise had no large community choir. On rare occasions, various church choirs would offer a public concert. However, with the notable exception of St. John's Cathedral, where Bishop Alphonsus Glorieux took pleasure in directing its choir, the church choirs were generally very limited in size and repertoire.

That all changed in October 1911, with the founding of the Boise Choral Society. While the official organizers were the Boise school district and the

Fig. 17: Boise Choral Society in concert, c. 1912. (ISHS)

Columbian Club (an influential "ladies' association"), there was never any doubt about Wesbrook's role as leader. In the first published description of the Society, Wesbrook stated it aimed to encourage a "higher musical atmosphere" as well as "unite the musical forces in the city." Those motives would eventually tend to be incompatible, but Wesbrook and the original members of the Boise Choral Society managed to hold them together without noticeable stress.

Far from being a gathering of the elite, the 100-150 singers included "most of the vocals in the city," according to the *Statesman*, ranging from those fully trained to musical novices. Yet, thanks to Wesbrook's directorial skills, they offered very ambitious programs (*figure* 17). The first concert, on Jan. 2, 1912, included a wide variety of selections from composers such as Gounod, Haydn and Rossini. Thereafter, they performed large-scale oratorios, beginning with Mendelssohn's Elijah in June 1912, and Handel's "Messiah" in June 1913. That marked the very first time Boiseans heard "Messiah," and it launched a tradition of annual performances of that masterpiece that continues to this day.

MUSIC WEEK

Although Arthur Wesbrook left Boise in mid-1914, his departure did not spell the end of the Choral Society,

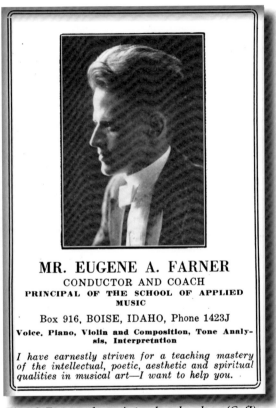

MR. EUGENE A. FARNER
CONDUCTOR AND COACH
PRINCIPAL OF THE SCHOOL OF APPLIED MUSIC

Box 916, BOISE, IDAHO, Phone 1423J

Voice, Piano, Violin and Composition, Tone Analysis, Interpretation

I have earnestly striven for a teaching mastery of the intellectual, poetic, aesthetic and spiritual qualities in musical art—I want to help you.

Fig. 18: Farner ad, music teachers brochure (CofI)

thanks to the leadership of L. W. Ensign. A local insurance executive and a bass soloist with the chorus, Ensign brought to bear organizational talents that

benefited a long list of musical groups until his death in 1936. Ensign not only held things together after Wesbrook's departure, but he articulated a whole new vision for the Choral Society. As he put it in September 1915: "[I]f we do not take steps at once in this matter, Pocatello or Nampa will be recognized as the musical center of the state." He was referring to a week-long musical festival Pocatello had begun the previous spring. It would be three and a half years before Boise responded to Ensign's challenge, but the result—Music Week—has played a crucial role in the history of Boise's music since then.

Eugene Farner (*figure* 18), commonly credited with founding Music Week, had become fully involved with the Choral Society by 1915, directing its orchestra in the January concert and a portion of the chorus in its production of Coleridge Taylor's operetta, "Kubla Khan," in December. Farner had come to Boise in 1912 to teach violin and voice at St. Margaret's Hall (an Episcopal girls' school) and soon became the choir director at St. Michael's Episcopal Cathedral. He had been a child prodigy, giving his first violin concert at the age of 10, and had studied conducting with Gustav Mahler when he directed the New York Philharmonic. Farner was also a very restless spirit, eagerly taking on many different tasks. In 1914, he organized the second Boy Scout troop in Boise as well as staging Gilbert and Sullivan's "H.M.S. Pinafore" as a fundraiser for St. Luke's Hospital. By 1922, he would be directing the music at Immanuel Lutheran Church and conducting the orchestra at First Methodist Church, while continuing as organist and choir director at St. Michael's.

Clearly, Farner had the varied talents and apparently inexhaustible energy necessary to assemble a city-wide music festival as an annual event. The Boise Choral Society served as a base for Farner's plans and then ended its independent existence in the spring of 1917. In September, Farner issued a call for "every singing group in the city" to help form a new alliance. To make clear its purpose, it would be called the Civic Festival Chorus. According to the *Statesman*, its first meeting approved a "general plan covering the rendition of the free municipal Christmas 'Messiah' and cooperating with all those interested

in establishing an annual spring music festival."

Farner received an enthusiastic response, and Boise's first Music Week might have been in 1918. America's entry into World War I, however, resulted in a year's delay. "Farner Called for War Service" read the headline in

Fig. 19: Popular WWI song. (Internet)

the *Statesman* on November 23. That forced the rescheduling of "Messiah" to December 16 so that Farner could direct it just prior to his departure for military duty. This sheds light on what would otherwise be inexplicable: how Farner managed to put on the first Music Week less than three months after he returned

to Boise in February 1919. That could happen because the stage had already been largely set in the autumn of 1917.

WORLD WAR I – UNCLE SAM AS SONG LEADER

The influence of World War I on Music Week went far beyond merely delaying it for a year. The war elevated community singing — a pleasant but seemingly inconsequential activity, pre-war — to a premier national status. "It is just as essential," Gen. Leonard Wood said, "that a soldier know how to sing as that he should carry a rifle, and know how to shoot." Consequently, Eugene Farner and hundreds of other musicians joined the army to serve as song leaders in every military camp, both at home and abroad. Before long, civilian leaders decided that if it worked for the troops, it would also work for those at home.

In October 1918, the *Ladies' Home Journal* carried an article titled "All America is Singing with Uncle Sam as Song Leader." Typical of most states, Idaho's Council of Defense issued a press release urging the organization of a Liberty Chorus in every community, or at least in every county. "The nation's famous war songs should be sung" at all community meetings, the Council asserted—not only by the chorus but also by everyone in the audience (*figures* 19, 21).

Canyon County loyally fell in line, with Caldwell setting up its Liberty Chorus in September 1918 and Nampa following suit the next month. F.F. Beale had been designated the county's Liberty Chorus director, so he led both the Caldwell and Nampa choruses.

There is no evidence Ada County had a Liberty Chorus, but it had a level of patriotic fervor equal to its neighbor. Boise's July 4th celebration in 1918, for example, did not repeat the street dancing of the year before. Instead, it held a choral march from Columbia Park (which at that time occupied the block west of the Capitol) to Julia Davis Park, where Beale led community singing.

A New Era in Boise Music – the Tuesday Musicale and the Columbian Club

In February 1919, Eugene Farner returned to a Boise, fully ready to enter the new era heralded in 1910 by the Columbia Band in its fair week series. The new era did not simply push aside the old order, symbolized by Sherman House. It co-opted the old order and also absorbed at least some of its musical values. The social elite—represented by those ladies whose activities appeared in the "Society" sections of the local newspapers—felt compelled to open their doors to a much broader public.

Take the Tuesday Musicale, for instance, founded in 1915 and in 2012 the longest-lived musical organization in Boise. Typical of the old order, its charter members resolved to keep their club very exclusive: The membership would be limited to the original 12. For the first two years, no report of its meetings appeared in the *Statesman*. The Musicale soon opened up, however, publically announcing its programs.

In May 1918, its Ladies Chorus, directed by F.F. Beale, gave a concert to benefit the Red

Fig. 20: Columbian Club (ISHS)

Cross. Nor was this merely a concession to wartime enthusiasm. The Ladies Chorus, later renamed the Choristers, has remained active to the present day.

On the other hand, neither Farner nor the other leaders of the Civic Festival Chorus showed any inclination to "play to the galleries" by limiting the Music Week program to popular songs. Instead, for its first production following Farner's return, the Chorus performed "The Redemption," an oratorio by Charles Gounod, at Easter services in First Methodist Church.

If Sherman House can be taken as the architectural symbol of the old order, then the new era's equivalent was not the band shell in Julia Davis Park but the Columbian Club (*figure* 20), where a wide variety of public performances would be staged during the 40 years of the building's existence — always with a decorous concern for the "good taste" to be

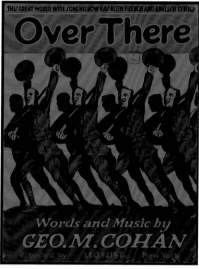

Fig. 21: "Over There" - popular WWI song (Internet)

expected of the ladies who made up its membership.

These, then, were the antecedents of the tradition of music provided by and for the people of Boise – what may be called "Boise Pops."

Fig. 22: "Hi Life," Boise High
School Courier, 1931 (ISHS, BHS)

If You Can't Sing, Holler

COMMUNITY SPIRIT AND THE BOISE POPS

Music Week dominated the musical scene in Boise throughout the 1920s.

What happened during that week each May overshadowed virtually all other

performances during the year.

Only the most extraordinary events, such as when John Phillip Sousa brought his band to town in 1926 and again in 1927, could match the local attention given Music Week. And yet the primary purpose of that annual festival was neither pure entertainment nor to showcase the most outstanding performers. Rather, what its leaders most wanted was maximum public involvement. The culminating event for each of the first 10 Music Weeks was a lantern parade (*figure* 23), concluded by community singing. "The idea," Eugene Farner told the *Statesman*, "of the 'promenade of lights' is simply to try and imbue Boise with the community spirit," so everyone needed to join in the singing. As Farner called out to the crowd in 1920, "If you can't sing, holler." This was the spirit of Music Week, the same spirit born when the Columbia Band played that cold, cold October in 1910 at the corner of Ninth and Main.

Although thousands of people had a good time attending Music Week events, it was actually very serious business. Music Week played, according to a remarkably unanimous consensus among the city's leaders, an essential role in "making a united people within a community," to quote a *Capital News* editorial. And "it is as participants," the 1920 Program argued, "not as spectators that the citizens of the community give true expression to community spirit." To reinforce the point, the 1921 Program quoted Walt Whitman: "I See America Go Singing to Its Destiny." No wonder Music Week had no trouble persuading the city's leaders to serve on its board of directors. Far be it for them to be left behind as the public went singing to the city's destiny. Consequently, the board for the very first Music Week included the mayor, members of the City Council, presidents of the Rotary and Commercial clubs, and several prominent business and professional men. That, in turn, assured the continuing existence of Music Week in the years to come. Individual musicians might come and go, including Farner after 1923, but the leaders of the city remained committed to the continued success of Music Week.

NOT FLAPPERS BUT MUSICIANS

While the Music Week board during the 1920s was composed largely of men, women also took on an important new role during those years. Not as flappers, however. Most people today tend to think of the 1920s as being the Jazz Age, symbolized by flappers dancing the Charleston. But one finds very little jazz in Boise before 1930.

Fig. 23: Scouts hold Music Week lanterns. (ISHS)

The 1923 "Jollies," a show staged by the local Shriners, included a chorus line dressed in flapper style, but jazz really didn't make it to Boise until the 1930 showing of "King of Jazz," a movie featuring Paul Whiteman and his orchestra. Consequently, the Music Week logo in the 1920s looked nothing like the drawing of "Hi Life" (*figure* 22) that appeared in the 1931 *Courier* (the Boise High School annual). Instead, it portrayed a rather feminine Pan (*figure* 25.)

Fig. 24: Kathryn Eckhardt Mitchell (left) string quartet (Bratt).
Fig. 25: Music Week logo, program cover, 1927. (ISHS)

The women who became important in the 1920s didn't look much like Pan, but they were definitely musicians, professionally trained and quite capable of earning their living playing music. Some grew up in Boise, such as Kathryn Eckhardt Mitchell (*figure* 24). A talented violinist, she began playing at society functions while still a teenager, but refused to be limited to such venues. After studying on the East Coast, she formed a piano trio that occasionally played at Kelly's Club Café and advertised its availability for "Banquets, Weddings, etc." However,

she soon chose to become a music educator and began teaching at the College of Idaho in 1926. Eckhardt Mitchell returned to New York City in 1929, graduated from what later became the Juilliard School (possibly the first Boisean to do so) and became one of the first music instructors at Boise Junior College.

Other women, such as Judith Mahan (*figure* 27) and Bernice Brusen (*figure* 26), came from elsewhere and remained in Boise for many years. Only a little can be

found on Mahan's background, but we know she arrived in Boise in 1922 and directed music in the elementary schools until the late 1940s. Proof of her skill at exciting children to perform can be seen in a number of Music Week Programs. School Night in

1923 included a pageant by Washington School students; in 1924, the Lowell School Boys chorus performed; and in 1926, Mahan chaired the School Night program.

Brusen gained an even larger role in Music Week, eventually rising to become the general chairman four times between 1938 and 1943. After completing her college education, she returned to Boise in 1926 to teach piano at St. Margaret's School (which she had attended) and taught privately after that school closed in 1932. She also maintained a remarkably full record of Music Week activities. Our knowledge of the history of Music Week is heavily dependent upon the Brusen and Music Week collections at the Idaho State Historical Society.

These musical pioneers in the 1920s— Eckhardt Mitchell, Mahan and Brusen, as well as others—broke the trail for a

Fig. 26: Bernice Brusen (ISHS)

Fig. 27: Teachers; Judith Mahan, standing, second from right. (ISHS)

Fig. 28: Music Week program, 1922 (ISHS)

long line of women teachers and administrators who shaped the development of music in Boise.

SUNDAY MUSIC

Most of Music Week's programming varied from year to year, but from the very first and continuing long

thereafter, it always began on a Sunday. Most churches scheduled special music for their morning services on that date and, beginning in 1922, the Municipal Band opened its season with a concert on that Sunday afternoon. There was nothing particularly innovative about the band concert. Boiseans had long been accustomed to its free, open-air concerts, although the attendance that first Music Week Sunday in 1922 was unusually large: estimated at 3,000. And the days of band member anonymity were definitely gone. The program named all 53 musicians.

Music in the churches, on the other hand, marked a significant departure from previous customs. Of course, most churches had music as part of their worship services, and the larger churches occasionally provided space for a concert, such as "Messiah" by the Civic Festival Chorus at First Methodist Church. Prior to Music Week, however, rarely did the churches offer public concerts unrelated to their religious mission.

Eugene Farner at St. Michael's

Episcopal Cathedral can be credited with initiating this new concert life in the churches. He assembled a large boys choir, which continued to perform long after he left Boise (*figure* 29). St. John's Catholic Cathedral soon followed suit, with F. F. Beale appointed its organist and choir director in September 1920. Over the next several years, he developed a music program for St. John's unmatched by any other Boise church (*figure* 30). In October 1925, for example, he offered an organ recital assisted by Judith Mahan, soprano, and Mrs. Mabel Woodcock Pittinger on violin. Two months later, St. John's gave a New Year's Eve concert featuring its own 20-piece orchestra, which had been organized the previous year.

The churches' music programs ranged over a wide gamut. Some were definitely sacred in character. Others lacked any apparent religious overtones, such as the Ladies' Rainbow Orchestra (a saxophone band) at First Congregational in 1924, a Scandinavian hand-bell group at First Christian Church in 1926, or a Beethoven trio at St. Michael's with

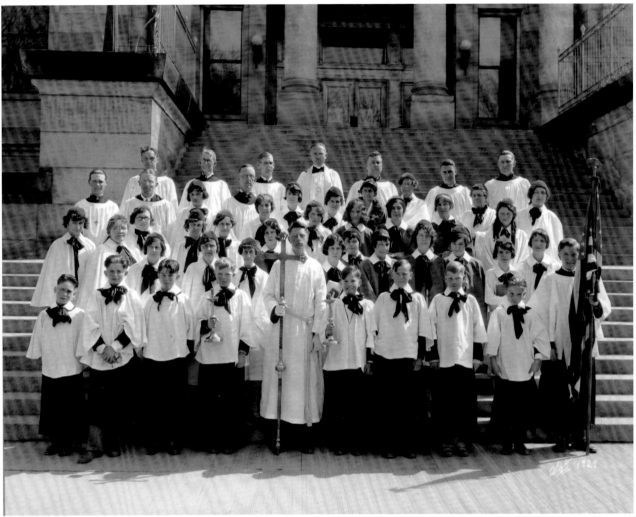

Fig. 29: St. Michael's Episcopal Cathedral Boys Choir, 1929. (ISHS)

James Strachan at the keyboard, Kathryn Eckhardt on violin and Catherine Ames on cello. In any case, they were offered without any noticeable rivalry. Thus, in September 1923, First Baptist invited St.

Michael's organist to inaugurate its new organ, while a month later Mrs. Laurel Elam, organist at First Methodist, gave a concert at St. Michael's.

Starting Music Week on Sunday

clearly revealed the city's leaders' intentions. While they wanted everyone involved, they also wished to set a certain tone for the whole week. By encouraging the public to be in church in the morning and then assemble in the afternoon for a band concert filled with innocently enjoyable tunes, they hoped to minimize the chance of anything that might be considered risky or even daringly unconventional.

Fig. 30: St. John's Catholic Cathedral, interior. (ISHS)

SETTING THE STAGE

Presenting Music Week forced its leaders to meet three major logistical challenges. In the first place, how would they pay for it? Other than the Municipal Band, which the city compensated, all of those involved worked for free, negating any need for a payroll. Nevertheless, there remained unavoidable expenses,

such as printing charges for several thousand copies of the program. In later years, the programs sported covers in full color, but even a run of the much more modest programs provided in earlier years (*figure* 28) cost several hundred dollars. Initially, the board sold season passes for each of the first two Music Weeks. Even though they cost only $1, that still conflicted with the goal of providing free admission. Therefore, beginning in 1921, the board relied on

small gifts from a large number of people. On Tag Day (the Saturday prior to the start of Music Week), 200 volunteers canvassed the city for pocket-change contributions. This system, which yielded $1,000 to $2,000 each year, met most of the festival's expenses until 1933, when the Community Chest (the forerunner of our present-day United Way) began paying the tab.

Having met the challenge of funding Music Week, the board still faced the need for an acceptable venue. Those planning each Music Week aimed to attract thousands, and yet the largest indoor site—even after the Boise High School Auditorium was rebuilt in 1922—seated only about 1,500. Besides, most people preferred open-air performances. The solution? Build a temporary stage in what is now Steunenberg Park. This allowed the audience to use the Capitol steps as an amphitheater (*figure* 1). The city agreed to pay the $1,000 per year to build the stage, which served up to 5,000 spectators for each night's performance. The high school auditorium was used in response to inclement weather until 1942, when the city withdrew its funding for the stage. Forced to hold most of its performances indoors significantly altered the character of Music Week thereafter. No longer could thousands be accommodated for a single performance. Not until 1959, when Music Week began producing a Broadway musical for several days, was it able to create a real equivalent to the broad appeal of the outdoor stage.

Selecting the precise dates each year for Music Week always proved to be a daunting task, involving a tug of war between early May and mid-summer. Because the schools always played a vital role in Music Week, their calendar suggested early May. Considering the chances for favorable weather, on the other hand, emphasized late June to mid-July. Until the 1950s, the schools won the tug, so Music Week occurred as late in the school calendar as possible, which usually meant the last week in May.

THE MAIN EVENT

Music Week programming during the 1920s strongly suggests that Eugene Farner and his associates wanted a large-scale production as the centerpiece of each year's performances. The Civic Festival Chorus included a great many singers—162, according to the 1920 Program—and it needed something quite ambitious to display its strengths. Furthermore, the whole aim of this annual festival, as the *Statesman* phrased it in 1919, was "to make the oratorio production and music and pageantry week a big thing in the life of Boise." For at least some people, that meant reinforcing traditional values. In the day of "jazz habits and jazz music," Gov. Charles Moore proclaimed in 1924, "the Boise festival chorus rises above this...to give us an appreciation of the finer, better things of life." Even in 1919, when the organizers had less than three months to pull together the first Music Week, they avoided the easy alternative of scheduling a random mixture of various groups and offered Gounod's "Redemption" as the year's centerpiece.

As long as Farner remained in charge, each Music Week did, in fact, include

a centerpiece. In 1920, it did not come from the Civic Festival Chorus, but from Haydn's "Creation." Performed by Boise High School with a chorus of 125 voices, it certainly served as an impressive substitute. In 1921, the Civic Festival Chorus returned, performing von Weber's "Jubilee" along with an oratorio celebrating the 300th anniversary of the Pilgrims' landing at Plymouth. As an added feature, the Chorus included participation by the Meridian Civic Chorus and the Eagle High School Glee Club. The following two years marked a high point in Music Week history, with the production of two operas. Gounod's "Faust" in 1922 (*figure* 31) included a chorus of 150 as well as ballet dancers and several tableaux. The performance lasted two and half hours. The audience of 5,000 stayed the course and vigorously applauded the performers. "Faust" has been repeated on numerous occasions over the years in the Boise area, but Tchaikovsky's "Eugene Onegin," the 1923 opera, has never since been performed locally.

Following Farner's departure later in 1923, the Music Week board found it difficult to find a replacement who possessed his skills as both producer and director. In 1924, the Civic Festival Chorus merely offered a selection of songs, surely a letdown after the dazzling performances of "Faust" and

Fig. 31: "Faust" chorus, Music Week, 1922 (ISHS)

"Eugene Onegin." The Chorus did mount oratorios in the next two years — Honegger's "Joan of Arc' in 1925 and Mendelssohn's "Walpurgis Night" in 1926 — but neither managed to capture the performance values of Farner's years. The board fell back on centerpieces by out-of-town groups in the last three

years of the 1920s. A Nampa choral group performed Handel's "Belshazzar" in 1927, with a cast of 100 including a chorus of 60. That marked the end of large-scale choral works, except for Part III of "Faust" on Nampa Night in 1929. The last two years of the decade featured the Pocatello Symphony Orchestra. Failing the development of a continuously functioning symphonic organization in Boise, Music Week supporters warmly welcomed Pocatello's, with a record-breaking attendance of 7,000 at the 1928 concert. "We've long had a good band," the *Statesman* wrote in a defensive editorial. "A good string section is all that we need to make the Boise band an acceptable if not exceptional symphony orchestra." The fact remained that Boise could not muster "a good string section," so Music Week fell back on a wide variety of other musical groups to fill out the programming for each year.

SUPPORTING ACTS

The musical performances filling out the rest of each Music Week varied greatly from year to year. Nevertheless, it's fair to say they were primarily choral, depended heavily on school children for performers, and showed a great readiness to reach out and be as inclusive as possible. The program for Tuesday, May 31, 1922, can serve as a good example. Being Memorial Day, it stressed patriotism. The evening began with the Tuesday Musicale Ladies Chorus, followed by the Boise High School Boys Glee Club, the Boise Valley Fife and Drum Corps and a girls' chorus from the YWCA, and concluded with a pageant staged by high school history students.

The element obviously missing from that program — and from much of Music Week during the 1920s — was orchestral. Planners hopefully included an Orchestra Night, and sometimes the Boise Concert Orchestra furnished symphonic music for the occasion. It never performed, except for Music Week, but sometimes met that challenge. In 1923, it filled its evening with a program including Schubert's "Unfinished

Symphony." The next year, however, it played only four selections, leaving the balance of the evening to the Ladies Chorus, and in 1926 it did not perform at all. The resulting gap might be filled by the high school orchestra, which played Grieg's "Peer Gynt Suite" in 1924, or even by a combined elementary school orchestra (*figure* 2, *pg ii*), but the appearance of the Pocatello Symphony in 1928 gained an enthusiastic local welcome.

Music Week planners dealt with the paucity of orchestral music by rounding up other types of instrumental offerings. There was the Boise Boys Band (replaced in 1929 by the American Legion Boys Band, *figure* 32). In 1926, Frederick

Fig. 32: *American Legion Boys Band, 1929. (ISHS)*

Fig. 33: Basque dancers, c. 1951. (ISHS)

Boothroyd, organist at St. Michael's, directed four grand pianos for the program of "Favorite Old Songs." In the following years, the group expanded to become an Eight Piano Symphony, which performed periodically for several decades thereafter.

The effort to be inclusive could have highly mixed results. Massed choruses of young school children—totaling 500 in 1921—always received warm applause, even if they were obviously far from professional in their performance. Also on the positive side were the chimes ringing from St. Michael's (only a few hundred feet from the Capitol stage). In 1926, to celebrate the installation of Boise's first carillon, they were played each evening prior to the opening of the regularly scheduled program. Those preludes probably seemed musically consistent to most of the audience, but one would have to wonder about the reactions the following year when the Boise banjo band played for half an hour immediately prior to the presentation of "Belshazzar," Handel's solemn oratorio.

Music Week's willingness to include activities beyond the strictly musical ranged most of the way from the sublime to the ridiculous. Dancing, for example, commonly found a place on the program from the beginning. As we have seen, the production of "Faust" in 1922 included ballet dancers. In 1927, on Saturday prior to the lantern parade, the evening was devoted to "Interpretive Dancing," to the evident pleasure of everyone. On the other hand, it could prove difficult to keep a clear focus on the festival's goals. In 1925, for example, the local polo team, then enjoying regional fame for its winning ways, asked to be allowed to lead the lantern parade. Local boosters quickly expanded on the idea by suggesting addition of other organizations, such as the El Korah Shrine Patrol and the Elks drill team. The *Statesman* thought this would "add to the picturesqueness and beauty of the scene." In fact, it threatened to overshadow the children in the lantern parade and was quickly abandoned.

BASQUES AND BLACKS

Music Week planners soon confronted barriers to inclusiveness, barriers arising from cultural as well as technological factors. To see how the prevailing local culture could limit inclusiveness, one need only compare and contrast the roles played by local Basques and blacks in Music Week programs.

Ethnic distinctiveness could result in either local appreciation or be the basis for de facto segregation. The Basques clearly enjoyed the former. Although Boise's Oinkari Dancers did not gain national acclaim until much later, beginning with their appearance at the 1964 New York World's Fair, the vivid attractions of Basque dancing, with its lively movement and colorful costumes (*figure* 33), had already gained local acceptance and even applause by the time of the first Music Week in 1919. The final night included what the *Statesman* called "bewitching dancing" in a program entitled "Dances of Many Nations." Although the Basques would have to tolerate for some years to come the obtuse local tendency to refer to them as "Spanish," they did manage to avoid the fate of the tiny local Chinese community, which could only watch an "Oriental dance" performed by Miss Ora Thornton. The 1927 Program included dancing of "La Jota" by two girls with recognizable Basque names, Juanita Uberaga and Matilda Anduiza. Far from suffering discrimination for their distinctive culture, the Basques were cherished by many Boiseans for giving the city its very own folk dancers. By 1938, they would be featured on the cover of the Music Week Program (*figure 34.*)

The experience of the Boise black community could scarcely have been more different. Even though it had been generally understood for most of the 20th century that popular American music owed an immense debt to the influences of black musical tastes and styles, Boise's blacks

Fig. 34: 1938 Music Week cover (ISHS)

had to await the arrival of jazz pianist Gene Harris in 1977 and the growing appreciation by the 1990s of black gospel music as performed at St. Paul Baptist Church before they could begin to break away from the discrimination clearly prevalent in the Music Week programs. During the 1920s, black people and not black music were shunned. In May 1924, for example, the Columbian Club heard a program of Negro spirituals by local performers who were apparently white. Proof that the issue involved the blacks themselves, not their music, can be seen in the brief inclusion of blacks in Church Night programming. They made their first appearance in 1924 with a quartet as well as the Bethel AME (African Methodist Episcopal) church choir. The following year, the Program noted the title of the selection "which was so popular" the previous year. The choir in 1925 caused the *Statesman* to declare "African Church Scores Success of Evening." Their performance brought "salvos of applause," and the audience demanded an encore. Did that lead to a continuing place for black music during Music Week? Far from it. The 1926 Program simply listed the Bethel choir selection as "Negro spiritual," and that was the last year it appeared at all. One should probably conclude that the white singers in other church choirs refused to be outshone by the blacks.

Segregation as practiced in Boise did not mean that black music was suppressed. As long as the blacks performed by themselves, they found a ready audience. In May 1926, for instance, Bethel AME church performed a musical, "Inspiration," directed by Lena Johnson, a prominent black singer from Tacoma, Wash. Both local papers gave substantial coverage to the preparation of the program, and it gained a full house at Boise High School Auditorium. The *Statesman* review found "the full rich negro voices blended beautifully in the musical numbers." However, no whites performed in "Inspiration," and that performance did nothing to gain black participation in white festivals, including Music Week. Eventually, of course, that would all change, but more than 50 years passed before segregation in Boise music began to wane.

RADIO: BOISE POPS HITS THE AIRWAVES

Music Week may have been lamentably slow integrating blacks into its programs, but radio offered such great opportunities for audience expansion that Music Week planners quickly began considering broadcasting its programs. The board discussed the idea in September 1927. That was barely five years after KFAU, the Boise High School radio station, had made the first musical broadcast in Idaho. Technical difficulties marred some of the early programs with a lot of static, but local radio enthusiasts persisted, and by

1924, St. Michael's broadcast all three of its Easter services. Music Week did not, in fact, broadcast its performances. "Why Not Radio the Concerts?" asked a 1928 *Capital News* editorial. The answer should have been obvious. Technical challenges posed by open-air performances were simply too great to be overcome in the 1920s. Broadcasters produced some rather impressive indoor programs, however. In January 1929, for instance, KIDO carried the 125-voice choir from Northwest Nazarene College, accompanied by a 20-piece orchestra, performing in an indoor concert hall. It would be well into the 1930s before local radio stations could cover outdoor concerts, and that decade, dominated by

the Great Depression nationally, proved to be quite a different time. Nevertheless, Music Week during the 1920s set a pace and created a popular following that would greatly influence the character of Boise's musical life for many years thereafter.

chapter

3 Fending Off Depression

"MUSIC IS AN ENEMY OF FEAR"

The Great Depression slammed into the American economy in October 1929, throwing it into a tailspin continuing well into the 1930s. However, Boiseans tended to see their home territory as being cushioned from its harshest aspects, and there is substantial evidence that the breadlines, bankruptcies and panic-stricken anxieties sweeping most of the country were mercifully muted in Boise.

Fig. 35: Francis Barnard in "Fatima," 1933. (C of I)

In any case, Boiseans relied on music to keep up their good spirits. As the Statesman put it in May 1932, "music is an enemy of fear."

That came in an editorial praising the Municipal Band's decision to boost local spirits by parading down Main Street on a Saturday afternoon. Band director George Flaharty reasoned, "Bands played during the war to cheer people and I'm sure the idea will work again."

Reinforced by parades a few days later by the Boise High School band (*figure* 36) and the American Legion Drum and Bugle Corps, these performances hearkened back to the tradition initiated by the Columbia Band in 1910, demonstrating that the Boise Pops remained alive and well even in the face of nationwide gloom.

The Boise Pops reflected a far wider consensus than simply a few dozen band members, as can be seen in the way Boise responded in July 1930 to the unparalleled opportunity to host the Passion Play touring the United States from Freiburg, Germany. With

less than two weeks to get ready, local boosters erected a huge stage 200 yards wide at the Fairgrounds, assembled and rehearsed a 130-voice choir and gathered more than 200 "extras" to fill out the crowd scenes. While other cities might find themselves unable to rise to the occasion—the extremely short notice probably reflected a cancellation elsewhere—Boise mounted the three-day show and generated large audiences

Fig. 36: Boise High School Band, 1932. (ISHS/BHS)

(2,500 on opening night) willing to pay substantial admission fees to see the internationally renown performance.

Similarly, in 1931 Music Week responded to the cancellation of the Pocatello Symphony by adding a seventh day featuring Boise High School musicians. Despite drastic budget cuts, such as the 75 percent reduction in 1933, Music Week continued throughout the 1930s to mount colorful and lighthearted

shows typified by "Le Cafe Continental" in 1934 (*figure* 37).

THE CURTAIN DROPS ON OPERA

Boiseans managed to parry a good bit of the Depression's musical impact into new opportunities, but grave losses remained that had to be absorbed. The heaviest was the curtailment of opera when the national touring companies faced insuperable financial burdens imposed by the Depression. Those companies had been delighting Boise audiences since the 1890s, but the foul winds of the Depression blew most of them away. Opera, undoubtedly the most popular musical genre for the previous 40 years and more, never recovered the widespread support it had enjoyed prior to 1930.

Opera during its heyday had what we would today find an unimaginably wide appeal. Of course, it brought out the social elite. A "large and fashionable audience" applauded Donizetti's "Lucia" in 1896 and "All Society Welcomes Coming Grand Opera," trumpeted an April 1936 headline in the *Statesman*. It also gained the eager patronage of those who could afford nothing more than the cheapest gallery seats. "Madame Butterfly," presented in April 1916 by

the level of public interest in the Boston company's production.

Consequently, presenting opera involved minimal financial risks. For example, the local businesswomen's club sponsored the December 1926 appearance of the Manhattan Opera

a choice of three operas—"Madame Butterfly," "Pagliacci" or a new Japanese opera—probably no one was surprised with the preference for "Madame Butterfly." With the exception of Bizet's "Carmen," a perennial favorite ("fascinating, captivating, wicked,"

Fig. 37: "Cafe Continental," Music Week 1934. (ISHS)

the Boston Grand Opera company with a ballet corps featuring Pavlova, evoked a lineup for tickets that started at 3:45 a.m., a phenomenon unequaled in Boise until the arrival of superstars such as Kenny Rogers in the 1980s. The review, running to half a page in the *Statesman*, testified to

Company, and although the heavy costs involved totaled $2,800, the club ended up with a modest profit of $100.

Both the traveling companies and their Boise audiences preferred the tried and true in repertoire. When the Manhattan company in 1926 gave Boise

the *Statesman* dubbed it in 1909), and Gounod's "Faust," performances sharply focused on the works of Puccini, Verdi and other Italian masters. Nothing by Wagner ever appeared in Boise.

Prior to 1930, Boiseans never attempted to stage a full-blown grand opera with local talent. On a few occasions, locals did perform comic opera — "Erminie" in 1904, sponsored by Bishop Glorieux, possibly being the first — and they particularly favored those by Gilbert & Sullivan. Nevertheless, they took immense pride in the frequency with which major companies came to town, and they showered their favorite stars with passionate adulation. Several, including Madame Nordica, enjoyed the limelight in Boise, but none more so or for longer than Ernestine Schumann-Heink (*figure 38*).

MADAME SCHUMANN-HEINK

Boiseans fell in love with Schumann-Heink at her first local concert in 1904. The *Statesman* praised "her marvelous tones which she alone is capable of producing" and concluded she "demonstrated her right to be called the world's greatest contralto." Her preeminence in Boise opinion could be seen in the advertisement for her first return engagement in December 1906, headlined "The Most Marvelous Of All

Fig. 38: Mme Ernestine Schumann-Heink, c. 1904. (Internet)

Prima Donnas" without even mentioning her name. Every year or two thereafter, Schumann-Heink performed in Boise until 1930, when she was 69 years old, and she always received the most lavish local recognition.

Her talents may have been a bit exaggerated locally, but Schumann-Heink had already earned an international reputation by the time she first appeared in Boise. She sang at Wagner's Bayreuth beginning in 1896, at the Metropolitan Opera in New York regularly from 1898, and began issuing recordings in 1900, more than a dozen of which have been reproduced on CD and are still available.

What evidently charmed Boiseans, however, was not only her undoubted musical talents, but also her personal presence and accessibility. Between her visits, she granted long interviews on a vast range of topics from skin care to the state of American music, and those interviews were fully covered in the local press. The mother of seven children whom she always claimed came first in her priorities, she warmly responded to youngsters' adulation. During a visit to Boise in 1923, she received an invitation from a delegation of Boy Scouts to camp out with them at Smith's Ferry. Regretting that her crowded schedule did not allow it, she promised in a letter published by the *Statesman* to return the next year and join them at their summer camp. As it turned out, she never found the time to fulfill that promise, but Boiseans clearly enjoyed the unpretentious and motherly concern she had shown.

Fig. 39: Boise High School cast and orchestra, "Fatima," 1933. (CofI)

In recognition of Schumann-Heink's readiness to sing at veterans' hospitals in Boise as well as many other places, when she died in 1936 her passing was recognized by the American Legion and the Disabled Veterans. Splendid as that ceremony surely was, it also marked the end of Boise's love affair not only with Schumann-Heink but also with grand opera as a popular art.

"FATIMA"

One hope remained. Perhaps opera could still be sustained at the local level. That thought gained some plausibility with the Dec. 8, 1933, premiere of "Fatima," the story of Bluebeard's last wife, by students at Boise High School. Albeit an amateur production, it had a huge cast in full costume, carefully constructed sets, and accompaniment by a full orchestra (*figures* 39 and 41). Furthermore, the score was the work of experienced professionals, composed by F.F. Beale with libretto by Alice C. D. Riley, the author of many poems rendered into published songs with Beale's music. The idea for the opera originally came from Beale's publisher, Birchard and

Company of Boston. We know he had worked on the score for well over a year, since the Columbian Club heard an abbreviated version in January 1933. The reviewers lauded the final result. The music had "depth and beauty," according to the *Capital News*. "Here is authentic music," declared the *Statesman*, "by an authentic Idahoan...music that breathes the spirit of Idaho."

However, "Fatima" did not prove to be the key (*figure* 40) to local opera productions. Beale continued to fuss with his score and College of Idaho students presented a revised version in February 1937, but "Fatima" was never published. Other opera enthusiasts fared little better. Ruth and John Henry Phillips, who had had extensive opera experience in the East, came to town in 1936 and opened a voice studio with hopes of mounting local productions. The Phillips

Fig. 40: Program, key ad for "Fatima." (Cofl)

Studio flourished and offered numerous recitals. It did manage to present a few operettas, but never grand opera. After the touring San Carlo Opera Company presented "Aida" in 1935, Boise saw only four operas in the later 1930s. Boise Junior College (founded in 1932 and numbering only a couple of hundred students) produced "Faust" in 1935 and "Carmen" in 1937. The Madrigal Club performed "Carmen" in 1938 and "Martha" in 1940. Otherwise, local tastes for opera had to manage with occasional study programs by the Tuesday Musicale and a Listeners Club (organized by Potter Howard, elected mayor 1947-1951) that gathered each Saturday beginning in 1942 to hear the Met on radio. Not until the 1970s would Boise gain an ongoing opera association, the Opera Workshop, which later evolved into Opera Idaho.

FRANCIS BARNARD

Curiously enough, "Fatima" did have notable success in at least one regard.

Boise H.S. Fatima Dec 8 1933 — Pancake Song..

Fig. 41: Six ladies singing, "Fatima." (CofI)

It served as the launching pad for the first Boisean to achieve a national career in music. Francis Barnard, a senior at Boise High when he played Bluebeard in "Fatima" (*figure* 35), had debuted four years earlier as a bass soloist in the Civic Festival Chorus's performance of Haydn's "Creation."

Barnard not only had exceptional talent as a vocalist; he also had the stamina and commitment without which one could scarcely hope to succeed in the highly competitive world of opera. While pursuing his education, he returned annually to Boise to visit his parents and give a concert or two in his home town. Press coverage of those visits provides glimpses of his career. He attended the Cincinnati Conservatory of Music for three years, during which he performed in "Pagliacci" at the Conservatory and debuted with the Cincinnati Symphony in Strauss' "Salome." He then attended George Washington University while performing with the DC Civic Opera Company. By 1941, the *Statesman* referred to him as "Boise's claim to distinction in the musical world." He then moved on to five years of graduate work at the Juilliard School and began to sing solos with the New England Opera Theater.

His first big break came in the summer of 1948 when he sang in "Don Giavanni" with the Boston Symphony in the annual summer festival at Tanglewood in Lenox, Mass. However, he continued for several more years with the New England Opera, while occasionally teaching at Juilliard.

Barnard's achievement of international recognition came about almost as improbably as had his first lead role in opera 25 years before. He joined a very small company, the After Dinner Opera, which had only a handful of singers and no obvious claim to fame. However, the After Dinner received an invitation to the 1957 Edinburgh Festival in Scotland, and that led to a tour throughout Europe and a busy schedule in North America and elsewhere in the following years.

By that time Boise could claim other musicians of national note, including Judy Lynn Voiten with the Grand Ole Opry and Paul Revere and his Raiders in rock 'n' roll. But the fact remains that Boise's first nationally performing musician was an opera singer.

COMMUNITY CONCERTS

Boiseans at home showed every bit as much pluck as had Barnard in pursuing his career elsewhere. Since they faced a very sharp limitation in the number of touring musicians, thanks to the Great Depression, they formed their own booking organization to maintain an adequate flow of musical talent. Fortunately, they didn't have to start from scratch. A nationwide Community Concerts Association (CCA) had recently been developed. Begun in Battle Creek, Mich., by a Chicago manager, by 1931 the CCA had located its headquarters in New York City. The CCA started with

the assumption that any community of at least 10,000 population could afford to participate in its program. Boise, with fewer than 40,000 in its county, was comfortably above the necessary minimum and reportedly became the first city in the West to join CCA.

The local Community Concert Association, organized in June, 1931, started out confident.

Fig. 42: Jascha Heifetz (Internet).

Fig. 43: Jan Peerce (Internet)

"There is no doubt that the requisite number of tickets can be sold," the *Statesman* editorialized. The original organizers simply relied on the leadership and networking that had assured the continuance of Music Week. The first president was Lewis Ensign;

F. F. Beale served as one of the vice-presidents; and Judith Mahan turned out to be one of the most successful ticket sellers. Every group in town that had ever shown an interest in music, from the Altrusa Club to the Municipal Band and University Women, took an active part in ticket sales. Consequently, in 1931 and every year for decades thereafter, the ticket drive lasted only a single week and always met its goal: enough sold to fill the Boise High School Auditorium, where all of the concerts were staged. Admission was strictly limited to season ticket holders. To avoid haggling over relative attractions, the local organization announced the season's program only after the ticket drive had been completed. This meant that season ticket holders were committed to the basic idea of Community Concerts and relinquished any option of making choices among proffered programs.

Particularly in its early years, Community Concerts provided a surprising number of outstanding programs—primarily operatic vocalists, but also a few instrumental soloists. Of course, there were some musicians whose names have long since sunk into obscurity, and others, such as Nelson

Eddy in March 1933, who only became "name stars" later. Nevertheless, compared with Boise's experience prior to 1931, Community Concerts brought some remarkable talent, including violinist Jascha Heifetz (*figure* 42) in 1936 and again in 1941, and Jan Peerce (*figure* 43) and Marian Anderson, both in 1940. That was possible because the nationwide shortage of available bookings even for top talent during the Depression made them affordable for small cities such as Boise. Season tickets cost only about $2. Thus, the total revenue for the 1932/33 season of Boise's Community Concerts totaled only $3,005 and yet still ended with a balance of $173. As artists' fees escalated after World War II, Community Concerts' ability to attract outstanding musicians commensurately declined, but during the 1930s and early 1940s it provided most of the major concerts each year.

MUSIC IN THE SCHOOLS

Community Concerts, of course, supplied a mere handful of programs annually. With only a small number of other touring shows passing through town, most of the time the stage remained available for local talent. Much of that turned out to be the product of the schools, and it was far more than the clichéd run of cute

Fig. 44: "Singing and Dancing Around the World (Germany)," Whittier School, Music Week, 1934. (ISHS)

performances that pleased proud parents but were avoided by almost everyone else. Thanks to the dedicated work of a number of teachers under the leadership of Judith Mahan, "the music program in the schools," bragged the *Statesman* in December, 1932, "has a place for every youngster, no matter how tone deaf he or she may be... ." "A Mischievous Christmas Mouse" may serve as an example of what that could achieve. This operetta written by two teachers at Garfield Elementary School, which had won a national prize, had a cast of 300 from the first four grades (that is to say, most of the children in those grades at Garfield) and was performed at Boise High Auditorium in December 1933. No photos of that performance can be found, but the Historical Society has a number of photos showing the 1934 Music Week school program, entitled "Singing and Dancing Around the World." Each elementary school focused on a particular country, Whittier featuring Germany (*figure* 44), and the result was far from childish.

With so many children involved in music from the very earliest grades, the high school had a very large talent pool to supply its choirs, bands and orchestras. And they found large enough audiences to stage ambitious performance schedules each year. Formerly, a Boise High music

Fig. 45: Boise High School a capella choir, Capitol Rotunda, 1941. (ISHS)

performance tended to include brief presentations by most if not all of the different groups. That rapidly changed. In May 1934, the *a capella* choir for the first time presented its own concert. Within a few more years, its Christmas

concert in the Capitol Rotunda (*figure* 45) had become a nationally broadcast tradition. The school music programs not only created the opportunity to begin a professional career, as we saw in the case of Francis Barnard, but they also showcased many who would enrich local adult music groups. Thus, the leads in "South of Sonora," the Boise High operetta production in 1935, included Helen Bullock and Gordon Eichmann, both of whom went on to local music leadership roles (Bullock directed the Madrigal Club and Eichmann the Gleemen).

This schooling created the potential for near-professional quality musical shows. "Fatima" remained an isolated case of opera at Boise High, but by 1939 it had launched a long series of operettas—and, later on, Broadway musicals—that enjoyed community-wide, enthusiastic audiences. All that had remained was to gain a leader who knew how to put all of the elements together.

Kenneth Hartzler admirably fit the bill. Hired in 1937, originally as the high school band instructor, within a year he was also directing the *a capella* choir and the glee clubs. A young man from a small town in Iowa, Hartzler quickly demonstrated leadership and drive equal in importance for Boise to that of Arthur Wesbrook. Hartzler's chain of hits began in 1939 with "The Red Mill" (*figure* 46), sporting a chorus of 250, which so thrilled the audience that a repeat performance had to be scheduled. By 1941, the *Statesman* lauded him as the man "who brought amateur juvenile operetta to Boise in grand style." In Chapter 6, we will see that he did the same for adult Broadway musicals in the 1960s.

SINGING AWAY THE GLOOM

Many of those who had enjoyed singing in school sought ways to continue after graduation. That undoubtedly refreshed the numbers in church choirs, and it also led to the founding of several new choral groups in the 1930s, which set a pace followed by many others after 1945. Unlike the Civic Festival Chorus, which slowly waned away, the new groups were much smaller, each reflecting a fairly specific demographic segment of the community rather than attempting to encompass everyone. The Madrigal Club, founded in late 1932 and thus the first of these new groups, included young women similar to those who joined the Junior League. Virgie Innskeep-

Betty Marley, Roger Vining, Pat Young, Clary Frazer
Dick Carter, Muriel Rogers, Virginia Christensen, Bill Leeper

Leslie Schwiebert, Willard Cook, Bill Smith,
Clary Frazer, Robert Lynch

"YOU NEVER CAN TELL ABOUT A WOMAN," SANG THE GAILY COSTUMED CAST OF "THE RED MILL"

Fig. 46: Cast, "The Red Mill," 1939. (ISHS/BHS)

Tippett, its founder, said it aimed to provide a place where the members could sing something "other than church songs." The Madrigal Club in effect replaced the Tuesday Musicale Ladies Chorus, which Beale had attempted to resuscitate in 1931 and 1932. The 30 or so "young girls," as the *Statesman* referred to them, took on relatively ambitious programs, performing "Carmen" in 1938 and "Martha" in 1940. The 1940 Musical America yearbook named the Madrigal Club as one of the two most outstanding groups in Idaho (the other being the College of Idaho choir directed by Beale.) Having gone through several name changes, the group still exists as Sounds.

The Gleemen, in contrast, focused on hearty, melodic and widely popular songs. They also took pride in drawing from a wide range of occupations. On several occasions, the singers were listed not only by name but also according to the way they earned their living.

One might call the Gleemen a singing men's service club. Donald Foltz, the

Fig. 47: Elks Gleemen; Idaho Centennial program, 1963. (Johnson)

choral director at Boise High School, founded the group in 1934, modeling it after similar groups on the West Coast. The Gleemen went inactive soon after the onset of World War II but took on a new life after the end of the war as the Elks' Gleemen, led by Gordon Eichmann (*figure* 47).

Some groups never got beyond a single, initial hopeful concert. The tiny local black community, for example, in 1933 brought in Elmer Bartlett from Los Angeles to help them organize a chorus. Forty singers joined in for a concert at the First Christian Church on May 18. It was so well received by the 800 people in the audience that the group added a second performance on May 31. The *Statesman* praised the "sweet and natural voices" of the chorus, and Bartlett announced his plan for the chorus "to carry on permanently," but that was the last heard about a black chorus for several decades.

Probably the least remembered of all the many choral groups in Boise, the Mothersingers gave numerous performances throughout the Boise Valley and elsewhere in the region from 1934 until it disbanded in 1941. Led by Judith Mahan for its first two years, the 35 to 50 singers were older than those in the Madrigal Club, from a lower social echelon and began as a spinoff of the PTA. They sang for PTA groups, at lodge halls and for other occasions with little social cachet. Unlike the Madrigal Club and the Gleemen, the Mothersingers never appeared on Music Week programs, nor did the group gain fully favorable attention from the local press. Typical of the *Statesman*'s patronizing attitude, it described a concert in March 1938 as having "a pleasantly romantic theme abounding in lovely ladies and valiant knights."

Regardless of their varied memberships, repertoires and longevity, the new choral groups of the 1930s demonstrated that, far from being prostrated by the Great Depression, Boiseans managed to keep up their spirits throughout that decade. In fact, as those years advanced, Boise Pops showed a whole new inclination toward combining concerts with popular dancing. The Big Band Era came late to Boise, but by 1939, with the opening of the Miramar Ballroom, it definitely arrived.

Fig. 48: Sheet music, "Valley of the Sun," 1963. (Johnson)

Fig. 49: Isham Jones and His Orchestra, 1936. (Internet)

chapter 4

Dancing at the Miramar

THE BELATED ARRIVAL OF BIG BANDS

The swing rhythms of the big bands — those of Glenn Miller, Benny

Goodman, Duke Ellington and many others — have become such a cherished

part of American popular culture that it is hard to imagine a time when

people had no interest in them. Boiseans, however, were extremely slow in

catching on to those rhythms.

The first big band of any note did not hit town until July 18, 1936. It was Isham Jones and His Orchestra (*figure 49*)—better remembered after Jones' retirement as Woody Herman and His Hermits. Only three other "name" bands appeared in Boise prior to the opening of the Miramar Ballroom in June 1939.

In explanation, local pundits alleged, as they frequently did when confronted by local musical anomalies, that this reflected Boise's remoteness. We were too far off the beaten track, so the argument went, for us to attract big time entertainment. Yet by the summer of 1941, nationally known big bands were playing monthly at the Miramar, which suggests something other than geography had been involved in the previous years.

The big band sound came so late to Boise at least in part because jazz, the predecessor of swing for much of the country, never really made it here at all. Boiseans could hear jazz on the radio, on phonograph records and, by the late 1920s, in movies such as Al Jolson's "The Jazz Singer." However, judging from reports and advertisements in the local press, jazz was only rarely performed locally. Al Finelle and His California Syncopaters

Fig. 50: National Guard jam session, Polo Field, 1935. (ISHS)

offered "red hot rhythms" for three days at the Pinney in March 1932. Briefly in late 1934, the Plantation golf clubhouse named its lounge the Cotton Club (referring to the famous Harlem jazz venue). But nothing like a real jazz scene could be found until March 1937, when Jack Brill, a recent arrival from New York City, opened the Jolly Jammers Club on Saturday evenings in the Owyhee Hotel, "where musicians and guests provide the impromptu entertainment" after an evening of dancing.

No Generation Gap

Unlike the 1960s, when many youngsters and their parents sharply differed about rock 'n' roll, during the 1930s teenagers appeared just about as slow as their elders to catch on to swing. The *Courier*, Boise High School's yearbook, did not include any photos of a dance band until 1932. Not until 1936 did the dance band gain a place in the high school band concerts. Although the *Courier* for that year claimed it "jazzes up the students and the faculty members at most of the school dances," it looked more like the Pep Band (*figure* 51) than,

for example, a National Guard band showing off in a 1935 jam session (*figure* 50). Renamed the Symphonic Dance Orchestra in 1937, as late as September 1940 it played for a party honoring the school district superintendent and his wife at the Columbian Club. Throughout

Fig. 51: Boise High School Pep Band, 1936. (ISHS/BHS)

the 1930s, Boise High's dance band had enough musicians that it could have been called a big band, but, to quote the title of a song made famous by Ella Fitzgerald, "It Don't Mean a Thing If It Ain't Got That Swing."

Dancing and Listening

The challenge had almost nothing to do with the type of dancing to

be seen on the dance floor. It wasn't simply a matter of doing the jitterbug rather than a waltz. What jazz and then swing called for was to focus on *listening* rather than *seeing* as a primary response to dance music. Otherwise, it became a variety of pageantry, as had been seen in Music Week productions from its beginning in 1919. In those productions, the emphasis lay on the dancers, their costumes and movements, rather than on the music. Entranced by the sights of those dances, the spectators denied that the music had been forced into an anonymous background. "The quality of the music did not suffer in the least," according to the *Statesman* in 1933, "from the liberal application of atmosphere, which added, on the contrary, real zest to the interpretation."

Nevertheless, neither in that report nor in the many others on Music Week dancing productions, did the reporter give any detailed description of the music. "Gay Scenery Aids Program," read the headline in 1934. Still, no matter how gaily the dancers swung their partners, the show had nothing of what Ella Fitzgerald meant by swing.

JOE VOITEN

Community Concerts had demonstrated Boise could sustain an annual classical music series with nationally known artists. Perhaps that could also be true for big bands. Such a possibility proved to be the cue for Joe Voiten. Now remembered, if at all, only as the father of Judy Lynn, Miss Idaho of 1955, who made a career of touring nationally with Grande Ole Opry, Voiten deserves to be recognized in his own right as the first of a continuing line of local promoters who played a crucial role in bringing to Boise nationally popular musicians. Raised in Coeur d'Alene, he came to Boise in 1926 after studying at a business school in Spokane. He founded and operated

for 40 years Idaho Barber and Beauty Supply, played in a dance band part-time and, with several partners, built Riverside Pavilion, an open-air dance hall on S. 9th Street that was later roofed and is now known as the Mardi Gras.

Voiten's business records are unavailable, so we can only guess at his reasons for doing so, but in July 1936 he sponsored the appearance of Isham Jones

Fig. 52: Miramar Ballroom. (Internet)

and His Orchestra. Evidently unsure of how to market this show, Voiten split it up into two parts. On Saturday afternoon he scheduled a concert at the Boise High School Auditorium, followed by a dance that evening at the Elks Lodge (in what is now called Jefferson Place at 9th and Jefferson streets.) It had mixed results. The concert attracted barely half a house, but the dance ended up with Standing Room Only.

Undiscouraged, Voiten tried again, bringing Jimmy Dorsey and His Band to Boise on April 13, 1937. This time he got the format right: Combine the concert and the dance. He rented the recently built Boise High School Gymnasium, which had plenty of dancing room on the main floor and a balcony that could seat 2,500 for those who just wanted to listen to the music. Dancers paid $2.25 per couple, while balcony seats went for 35 cents (only 25 cents for students).

Dorsey and his group were such an obvious success that Voiten went for the biggest band of all. Paul Whiteman and his 25 musicians played at the Elks on Oct. 14, 1937. Voiten charged what must have seemed like astronomical prices to Boiseans at the time: $3.30 per person for admission to the dance floor or $1.10 for a balcony seat. But how could one quibble over prices? This, after all, was "the King of Modern Music." With his arrival in New York in 1920, the *Statesman* assured its readers, "America got its first taste of modern jazz."

Voiten's successes with Dorsey and

Whiteman may have blinded him to the risks in his new business. In any case, his next booking was his last—Fletcher Henderson and His Colored Swingsters on Jan. 22, 1938. All of the bands Voiten had previously brought to town had been white and could draw crowds even at high prices. Even by heavily discounting the tickets—$1.10 for men, 55 cents for ladies and 55 cents for the balcony in the Elks Ballroom—Voiten could not overcome prevailing racial barriers, and his career as a promoter ended. Nevertheless, he had clearly shown that a market existed for big-name big bands in Boise. Only one thing remained undone: Create a venue that could make a steady business out of responding to that market.

THE MIRAMAR BALLROOM

The Miramar (*figure* 52) staged its grand opening on June 28, 1939. Although eventually it became the most popular ballroom in Boise, hosting most of the best-known bands in the 1940s and 1950s, it had a very quiet opening. The advertisements stressed the availability of free buses from downtown, since it

was located a mile beyond the city limits (on Fairview, west of Orchard Street on the site now occupied by Alden-Waggoner Funeral Home). However, those ads made no mention of what band was playing. In fact, not until the spring of 1941 did its management bring in nationally known bands, beginning in March with Duke Ellington, followed by Fats Waller in July, Earl Hines in August and Paul Whiteman in September.

The name bands followed the completion of substantial remodeling in February 1941, and those improvements certainly enhanced its competitive advantage over other dance halls then existing in Boise. Dancing occurred in a variety of settings, including the Riverside, of which Voiten had once been a part-owner, and White City Park adjoining the Natatorium. But with the exception of the Elks Ballroom (which probably seemed too socially elevated for many ordinary Boiseans), none had space both for dancers and listeners. The Miramar's 1941 remodeling emphasized that difference, stressing the addition of a terrace that could accommodate up to 100 people.

The remodeling surely increased the management's willingness to venture

the money to bring in nationally known bands, but it doesn't adequately explain a whole new tone to the Miramar's promotion of those big bands. For example, Duke Ellington's entourage was advertised as "the world's greatest colored orchestra." An article in the *Statesman* emphasized the blackness of Fats Waller, titling it "Hey, Hey, You Cats, Boom!" with a portrait focused on his bugged eyes and wide-open mouth. What had happened to the racism that had so evidently spoiled Fletcher Henderson's appearance in Boise three years before?

GOWEN FIELD

Things had obviously changed, significantly enhancing the market for big bands and sharply reducing the racism that had so limited the acceptability of black bands in Boise. The most important change derived from a whole new audience, thanks to Gowen Field. The United States had not yet entered World War II, but Gowen Field was already bringing hundreds, eventually thousands, of airmen to Boise, many of whom came from metropolitan areas that had grown accustomed to the blackness of jazz musicians such as Duke Ellington and Fats Waller.

Like every other American city worth its salt, Boise had lobbied hard to gain at least one of the rapidly growing number of military installations being built as the nation moved toward a war footing. What it got was Gowen Field, a bomber training base occupying several thousand acres on the south side of the Boise airport. The new base sprang up with breathtaking speed. The Corps of Engineers design team began work in the first days of 1941. By the end of May, most of the facility had been erected, and the airmen soon arrived, hundreds more every month.

The airmen's recreational tastes certainly included music, predominately dance music, both as performers and as audience. By November 1941, the Jive Bombers were offering a free Sunday afternoon concert on the base, "a combination 'jam' and 'sweet swing' session." Two years later, the Gowen Field dance band staged an Armistice Day dance at the Miramar. It seems clear that throngs of airmen flocked to the Miramar on many other occasions, especially when nationally known bands were playing. This resulted in an influx of name bands unsurpassed in frequency until the 1980s: Jack Teegarden in May 1942, Lionel Hampton the following October and Tommy Dorsey (featuring Frank Sinatra as vocalist) in November. In 1943, Teegarden returned, and Jan Garber came in May, Louis Armstrong in July and Louis Prima in October. The market was so hot, even Fletcher Henderson made it back to Boise—in July 1944 and again in October.

The Miramar during the war years not only fostered a taste for jazz bands,

Fig. 53: Gib Hochstrasser. (Internet)

it also created an opportunity for young local musicians. As the war continued, the Miramar found it increasingly difficult to book touring bands; their musicians were being drafted into the military ranks. Consequently, the Miramar turned to local bands, staffed in some cases by high school students. That is how a 16-year-old high school student by the name of Gib Hochstrasser got his start. Initially playing in the Bud Finch Band, by 1944 Gib had become its leader. By war's end, Gib and his band played many Thursdays through Saturdays at the Miramar, launching him on a half-century career as Idaho's "King of Swing" (*figure* 53). Thus, dancing at the Miramar paved the way for a remarkable postwar surge of music in Boise. The time was now ripe for the Boise Junior College annual revue, "Bach to Boogie."

chapter

5

Fig. 54: Spike Jones album cover. (Internet)

"Bach to Boogie"

POSTWAR EFFERVESCENCE

The first years following the end of World War II saw an outpouring of musical excitement

in Boise unmatched before or since. For variety, performance values and widespread public

involvement, those years stand as a unique period in Boise's music history. It seemed like it

might last forever, but it passed away within 15 years; by 1960 quite a different musical scene

began to replace it.

Part of the musical excitement came from touring performers. The Miramar continued to draw major bands—Duke Ellington appeared annually between 1952 and 1955—and also broadened the type of music it presented, including Country & Western with Bob Wills and His Texas

Fig. 55: Leontyne Price (ISHS)

Playboys in 1947 and the "Champagne Music" of Lawrence Welk in 1949. Boiseans' taste for classical music not only sustained the Community Concerts, but supported the scheduling of operatic soloists such as Leontyne Price (*figure* 55) and ensembles like the Longines Symphonette (*figure* 56). It even provided a market for a second series, the Idaho Concerts and Artists managed by the Junior League, which brought Isaac Stern and John Charles Thomas to Boise in the 1947/48 season.

The word had evidently spread that Boise welcomed all kinds of music, and that brought performers of almost all sorts. After a long hiatus, the Boston Grand Opera Company returned in 1949 with "Carmen" and "La Traviata." At the opposite extreme from this high-minded seriousness, Spike Jones (*figure* 54) and "His Inanities" entertained an audience of 4,000 at Bronco Stadium in August 1953. Occupying an aesthetic midpoint, Country & Western pleased many

listeners. The Snake River Stampede in Nampa featured nationally known stars such as Gene Autry and the Sons of the Pioneers. A touring group from the Grand Ole Opry, including Boise's own Judy Lynn Voiten, appeared at Boise High School Auditorium in November 1956.

Pleased as Boiseans might have been to welcome Judy Voiten back home, they

Fig. 56: Longines Symphonette (ISHS)

had no need to depend on Nashville or anywhere else to provide most of their music performances. In those first postwar years, Boise saw and welcomed an amazing number and variety of local performers and musical groups. Some of the choral groups — including the Madrigal Club (*figure* 57), the Gleemen and the Tuesday Musicale Chorus (renamed the Choristers in 1953) — had originated in the 1930s and came back to life with peacetime. Others, such as the El Korah Shrine Chanters, had existed for many years but began offering public concerts only after the war. Then there were groups formed during the war, such as the St. Luke's Hospital nursing school choir, which continued into the 1950s.

Many others originated in the first postwar years. The Mormonaires, a 50-voice male chorus, began singing in 1949. The Kiwanis Boys Choir, modeled after the Vienna Boys Choir, which had performed in Boise in 1948, was organized at the end of 1951. Barbershop quartets rapidly gained popularity in the later 1950s. Prominent directors formed their own choirs. Probably the most unlikely, at least in name, was the Idaho Motor Transportation Association

Chorus, assembled by Kenneth Hartzler, at the time the managing director of the IMTA. Gordon Eichmann organized the Eichmann Ensemble, and David Wehr

Fig. 57: Madrigal Club, 1988. (Bivens)

formed his Symphonic Choral Society barely a year after his 1958 arrival in Boise. Some groups, such as the Boise Valley Singing Convention (dedicated to white gospel music), barely gained any public recognition at all.

Instrumental music also saw significant expansion. In addition to the continuing presence of the Municipal Band and large, well-trained school

bands and orchestras, many new groups appeared after 1945. The most important step for the future of music in Boise, of course, was the development at long last of a permanent symphony orchestra (which we will consider in more detail later in this chapter). Paralleling the emergence of the Boise Civic Symphony was the college community orchestra at Boise Junior College. For sheer fun, Boise enjoyed a rapid proliferation of groups as varied as oldtime fiddlers (*figure* 58), Bill Jamison's German band, and Louie Ventrella and Gib Hochstrasser's orchestra, which initiated in 1956 the tradition of "Jazz Under the Stars" in Julia Davis Park.

Although technically amateurs, these performers frequently gained regional and even national recognition for the quality of their concerts. Fern Nolte Davidson, a pianist from Nampa, played in Carnegie Hall in 1948, possibly the first Boise-area musician to gain that honor. Both the Choristers and the Gleemen won top places in national competitions. The Boise High School *a capella* choir's annual Christmas concert in the Capitol Rotunda was carried nationally on radio.

Very few of these groups continued into the 21st century. One might assume that the prospects for survival would be quite predictable—that a nursing school choir, for example, had a far smaller chance of enduring over the long haul than the Shriners' Chanters. However, the fate of three different groups demonstrates how unpredictable the musical scene really was in the early postwar period.

The revival of the Civic Festival Chorus might have seemed to be a sure thing. In February 1946, the Music Week board decided it was "an auspicious time," as Bernice Brusen put it, "to work toward American unity through music." As chairman of the committee organizing the Boise Civic

Chorus, Brusen apparently faced clear sailing. A chorus of 100 voices, drawn from various local church choirs, first performed during the 1946 Music Week. A few months later, the Chorus gained a strong conductor, C. Griffith Bratt, who had just come to town as the head

Fig. 58: Old-Time Fiddlers on float, Music Week parade, 1948. (ISHS)

of BJC's music program. Under Bratt's leadership, the Chorus performed admirably, and yet the membership slowly declined to the point that a "revamping" was announced in October 1950—and that was the last ever heard of the Boise Civic Chorus. Combining

church choirs, which had seemed so appropriate in 1917, proved unworkable in the 1940s. Not until the formation of the Master Chorale in 1975 did a sustainable alternative appear. If the time had passed for something like the Civic Chorus, it had not yet come for a permanent opera company.

Organized in June 1949, the Boise Opera Company could look back on the longtime popularity of opera in Boise. With the experienced leadership of John Henry and Ruth Phillips, who had taught operatic singing in Boise for more than 20 years, and the enthusiastic support of such talented singers as Stanton Stringfellow and Gordon Eichmann, it seemed a plausible time to launch that endeavor. The Company enjoyed very friendly press coverage from the *Statesman* and an appreciative audience of tolerable, if not huge, size. Nevertheless, after 18 months, it lapsed into silence, broken only by a well-received production of Menotti's "Amahl and the Night Visitors" at Christmastime in 1953. Not until the 1980s, when Boise had become a much larger city, did the Boise Opera Company reappear and grow into what is now Opera Idaho.

In dramatic contrast to the Civic Chorus and the Boise Opera Company, Boise Junior College (BJC) had the temerity to combine serious choral music with

Fig. 59: *Bach to Boogie, 1948. (Gib Hochstrasser, center; Bill Jamison, right) (Jamison)*

a slap-happy student revue. That highly improbable undertaking, called "Bach to Boogie," enjoyed remarkable success.

"BACH TO BOOGIE"

During the six years of its existence (1947-1952), "Bach to Boogie' offered a varied program, but each year it had the same general structure. It opened with the BJC choir, directed by Bratt, singing choral works by Bach.

Then followed a flamboyantly upbeat presentation of music and dance from periods since Bach's time, ending with jitterbugging (*figure 59*) to the "Bach to Boogie Bounce," composed by Gib Hochstrasser and performed by

his 20-piece dance band. The show turned out to be "mostly boogie," according to a reviewer

Fig. 60: *"Jug Huggers" (Bob Bakes, Buryl Carringer, Marvin Gardner, Mickey Ogan, Bill Johnston), Bach to Boogie, c. 1950. (Statesman/BSU Library)*

in 1948, "with very little Bach. Even so, Bach, himself, would have been enchanted." Certainly, Boiseans were. It proved such a hit that it was moved in 1948 from the small BJC Auditorium

to the much larger one at Boise High. It ended only after Gib graduated and moved on to other challenges, depriving the revue of its essential creative force.

Nevertheless, for all of its brief existence, "Bach to Boogie" stands as a near-perfect symbol of its time. That's not because it was unique in combining serious and popular music in the same program. That had been done before. (In June 1946, for example, the Municipal Band offered a program combining Beethoven and boogie. Played by a brass band, however, the music suffered a certain homogenization. "Bach to Boogie" avoided that by using different performing groups: Bach was sung by a choir while boogie was played by a swing band.) The unique characteristic of the show, and of its period, was its hearty celebration of widely varying musical traditions, and that reflected the personalities of its founders.

Bratt (*figure* 61) and Hochstrasser came from radically different backgrounds. Bratt received rigorous formal training as an organist, gaining a Master's degree from Baltimore's Peabody Conservatory. Hochstrasser, on the other hand, learned his music on the street. He gained his first notice in the *Statesman* in 1942 (a year before he joined the Bud Finch Band playing at the Miramar) as a tap dancer with an all-girl dance orchestra.

Despite the gulf dividing their musical backgrounds, Bratt and Gib recognized the strengths of each other's music and welcomed its results. To this day, Bratt fondly recalls Gib as one of his best students. That attitude, which rose above mere tolerance to positive enjoyment of cultural differences, gained lively expression from many of the participants in "Bach to Boogie." Among the students, Robert Bakes, later Chief Justice of the Idaho Supreme Court, could be seen playing in a hillbilly band (*figure* 60). Among the adults, Eugene Chaffee, the college president, joined three faculty members singing a quartet. That they did so in blackface probably would be viewed today as a sign of racism. At the time, it almost surely demonstrated the celebration of the longtime popularity of minstrel shows. That, in turn, reflected a rather bittersweet sub-text that "Bach to Boogie" shared with the culture of the early postwar years. Both the musicians and their listeners lived in an era when the morning after the concert included newspaper reports of the Cold War and the threat of nuclear conflict. Closer to home, the prospect of loss was far less nightmarish, but much more likely. While swing music had a much shorter history than Bach motets or minstrel shows, it too was rapidly becoming more of a memory than a living reality.

Fig. 61: C. Griffith Bratt. (BSU Library)

"CONCERTO TO A MEMORY"

While we don't know the subject memorialized by Gib Hochstrasser in his "Concerto to a Memory" (perhaps he was recollecting George Gerschwin's "Rhapsody in Blue" for Paul Whiteman's orchestra 20 years earlier?), the fact that he showcased it in the 1948 "Bach to Boogie" clearly suggests that he was far more than a showman. His obvious enjoyment of clowning for an audience (front and center in *figure* 58), did not in the least diminish his lifelong passion for musical composition. In 1987, he told a reporter "the one thing I did want to do through all of this...was to arrange, to write and arrange my own music."

It was a unique time to be a composer in Boise. Still a very small city, with a population of only 35,393 in 1950, Boise nonetheless had a remarkable number of composers, and they found a ready local audience for their compositions. Louie Ventrella, for example, premiered his own work in 1949 with his Boise Concert Orchestra, including "West Indian Serenade" and "First Rhapsody," but the Boise Civic Symphony later premiered his "Owyhee Suite." John Best, conductor of the BJC orchestra, premiered his own "Prelude in B Minor" in 1954.

Recognition could come very quickly.

In March 1959, a program presented by the Tuesday Musicale featured Idaho composers. Included among the seven selected was David Wehr, who had arrived in Boise less than a year earlier.

Some of these composers are utterly forgotten today. Take for instance George Dawson, a native Boise pianist. In February 1946, the Tuesday Musicale included him in a program on "ultra modern music." That might suggest his music was too experimental to gain performance. However, in 1952 the Boise Civic Symphony premiered Dawson's "Overture to a Tragedy."

C. Griffith Bratt was undoubtedly the most prolific and most widely known of the Boise composers, then and still today. Very early on, he had set a very demanding pace for himself. Prior to his arrival in 1946 he had already composed more than 100 different pieces. The bulk of them were organ and choral works for church use, but they also included his 1st Symphony, part of which he had composed while serving in the Navy. Even with a heavy teaching load at BJC and his time-consuming duties as organist and choir director at St. Michael's Cathedral, Bratt continued to produce numerous compositions—

even up to the present, when he is in his 90s. The 1951 premiere of his "Quintet in F Minor" indicated the respect his work received from local musicians, with James Hopper on clarinet, Stella Margaret Hopper and Henry Simonson

Fig. 62: Program cover (Neil)

playing violin, John Best on the cello and Henry von der Heide playing viola. Later highlights in this period of Bratt's career as a composer would have to include the commissioning of his 2nd Symphony by the Idaho Federation of Music Clubs, which premiered at BJC in April 1956. Its fourth movement contained a chorale sung by the Elks Gleemen. The

culmination came with his first opera, "A Season for Sorrow" (*figure* 62). Focused on Harry Orchard, the convicted assassin of former Gov. Frank Steunenberg, it was composed at the request of the National Federation of Music Clubs in observance of Idaho's Territorial Centennial. First performed in September 1962 in the Boise High School Auditorium (29 years after the premiere of Beale's "Fatima"), "Season for Sorrow" received six additional performances over the following two years. It was revived in 1990 during the observance of Idaho's statehood centennial.

PROFESSIONALISM AND PLAYFULNESS

No other Boisean produced an opera during this era, and very few local musicians could match Hochstrasser's talent for arranging music, but many shared Bratt's and Hochstrasser's commitment to a professionalism that included a playful approach to their art. Bratt had no trouble picking up on the creative improvisation so essential to jazz. For example, as a climax to his recital at BJC in October 1957, Bratt received a theme from George Dawson and proceeded to improvise five variations on it.

Other musicians expressed their playful approach to their music in different ways. Bert Burda, a choir director in Boise high schools who sang the lead in "A Season for Sorrow," also enjoyed singing with the Gem Dandies (*figure* 63), an award-winning barbershop quartet that included Gordon Eichmann and David Wehr. James Hopper, a Julliard-trained clarinetist who frequently appeared as a soloist with local classical music groups, thought it great fun to don lederhosen and join in with Jamison's German band (*figure* 64).

The German band had no elevated goal, simply striving to delight its audience with lighthearted fun.

Fig. 63: Gem Dandies, 1960 (Burda)

However, even as high-minded a group as the Boise Civic Symphony showed no embarrassment when it included "Pop Goes the Weasel" in its program for the spring of 1952. It is true that Henry von der Heide, the director of the symphony, used the selection in a youth concert to demonstrate the instrumentation of the orchestra, but it had already been played the month before for an adult audience. The lesson seemed clear enough: One could have fun even while performing classical music.

BOISE CIVIC SYMPHONY

I was during this unique era of musical creativity that Boise finally got its own symphonic orchestra. There had been several earlier attempts, dating back to 1906 with Mose Christensen and his Boise Symphony Orchestra and, most recently, Beale's Little Symphony in the mid-1930s. In each case, the effort started out with great hopes but then fizzled within a year or two. This time it not only got started, but actually managed to survive. Eventually, it became the Boise Philharmonic, which dominates the orchestral scene today.

The Boise Civic Symphony commenced with the arrival in October 1941 of Even Breyen. An itinerant conductor, something of an orchestral Harold Hill (portrayed in "The Music Man"), Breyen declared "we need good music more than ever to take away the gloom of world strife" and proposed the Boise Civic Symphony to meet that need. He seemed to have impressive credentials—a graduate of the Royal Conservatory of Music in Copenhagen, he had played in Victor Herbert's orchestra and organized several community orchestras in the Midwest. Nevertheless, several of Boise's leading musicians, including Kathryn Eckhardt Mitchell, spurned Breyen's invitation and quickly started the competing Boise String Symphony. While the String Symphony lasted less than a year, it came close to torpedoing Breyen's dream. During its brief existence, the String Symphony's performances included substantial portions of such masters as Mozart and Debussy, marking a sharp contrast with the light, even fluffy fare ("God Bless America" and Brahms' "Cradle Song," for instance) offered by the Civic Symphony. Breyen scrambled to obtain concert locations wherever possible, but gave it all up in January 1944. Albert Tompkins, a longtime local musician, took over as director, as he had on several similar occasions in the previous 30 years, but it seemed unlikely he would be able to keep the Civic Symphony going.

The crucial difference from earlier attempts to assure an orchestra's existence appeared in September 1944. A large group of Boise's business and professional leaders gathered for dinner at the Owyhee Hotel and "formulated,"

according to the *Statesman*, "a plan for the Boise Concert orchestra." The group appointed Reilly Atkinson, a prominent wholesaler and former Music Week board member, to head a committee to

Fig. 64: Bill Jamison's German Band. (Jamison)

flesh out the plan to keep the orchestra in business. In case anyone missed the point, the orchestra began in November to introduce its concerts by noting it had "the personal interest and backing of Boise business and civic organizations." The Boise Civic Symphony, and later the Boise Philharmonic, survived for a variety of reasons, including the quality of local musicians, but most importantly because community leaders have been committed to its success. The continuing

existence of Music Week for more than 90 years testifies to the importance of that kind of commitment.

The Symphony slowly grew in the second half of the 1940s, increasing the number of its musicians from 38 in 1945 to 63 in 1950. It frequently drew an audience of 1,000. The repertoire rarely included really challenging work, but avoided the saccharine character of Breyen's selections. The concert in February 1947, for example, included Bizet's "L'Arlesienne Suite" and selections from Puccini's "La Boheme." On the other hand, the October 1949 performance of Grieg's "Peer Gynt Suite" omitted one movement for lack of an oboe soloist.

Its well-wishers may have worried that the Boise Concert Orchestra, organized by Louie Ventrella in late 1948, might pose serious competition to the Civic Symphony. However, Ventrella's group, later renamed the Boise Symphonette and supported by the local musicians' union, found its place offering free summertime pops concerts in Julia Davis Park.

With the 1944 "plan," the Civic Symphony had an assured existence, but it needed a strong leader to get beyond survival mode. Tompkins retired in early 1949. William Sunderland, who had been playing in the violin section and had extensive experience as a conductor,

Fig. 65: Henry von der Heide (von der Heide)

replaced Tompkins but showed no immediate signs of strong leadership. That all changed in the summer of 1950, with the election of Paul Ennis as president of the board and its appointment of Henry von der Heide (*figure* 65) as musical director. Ennis began the rapid development of a strong support system, while von der Heide quickly jumped the orchestra into a far more ambitious mode of musicianship and repertoire.

Von der Heide had an electrifying effect on the Civic Symphony, reminiscent of Arthur Wesbrook's effect on Boise in 1911. This young man, not yet 30 years of age, from Owatonna, Minn., immediately dispatched the leisurely pace to which the Symphony had grown accustomed. He booked Fern Nolte Davidson, the Nampan who had recently made her second appearance in Carnegie Hall, to play Tchaikovsky's "Piano Concerto No. 1" and opened the season in November at Nampa's Central Auditorium. When Boiseans heard the concert the following evening, they were bowled over by a program that the *Statesman* reviewer declared "not before equaled by valley musical talent." While apparently new to Boiseans, von der Heide's recipe for program building followed practices commonly found in many established orchestras in the

Fig. 66: School Night concert, Boise High School gymnasium, Music Week c. 1950. (von der Heide)

United States: a judicious mixture of Haydn, Mozart, Beethoven and other standard classics with an occasional startling crowd-pleaser. Thus, in March 1951, he included Tchaikovsky's "1812 Overture."

In addition to initiating "run-outs"

Fig. 67: Map, 1953. (ISHS)

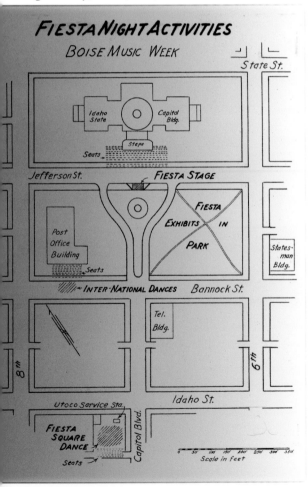

with the Nampa performance, von der Heide also began a number of other practices that became regular features on the Symphony's annual calendar and continue today. Beginning in September 1951, he announced the programs for the entire season, originally composed of three concerts and expanded to five a couple of years later. At least one of those concerts focused on youth, either as performers or for an audience composed of youngsters. Violinists Barbara Shook and Heidi Wayne, the first young local soloists, both went on to distinguished musical careers. The first Youth Concert included "Pop Goes the Weasel," as we noted earlier.

The pool of local talent was none too capacious, particularly for string players, and von der Heide also faced competition from the BJC orchestra. However, he met that challenge in two ways. Unlike Breyen, he managed to persuade some of the college musicians to join the Civic Symphony, including Kathryn Eckhardt Mitchell in September 1951. Von der Heide rewarded Mitchell by designating her as the soloist in the April 1952 performance of Bach's "Brandenburg Concerto No. 4." He also recruited talented high school students

such as Berta Jo Smith, who was still playing in the bass section in 2011.

All of this cost money, and von der Heide took an active part in coaching board members on how to do fundraising. In the first place, once one had a multi-concert season, season tickets should be sold. That began in October 1951, with the first ticket being sold to Gov. Len Jordan. Since the Symphony had no paid office staff, the Auxiliary was organized in January 1952. For several years, it did much of the office work as well as tasks more commonly associated with auxiliaries, such as planning and hosting after-concert receptions. The annual budget remained minuscule by latter-day standards. The fiscal report to the board in May 1954 showed annual revenues at $5,754 and expenses at $4,554, of which the conductor's salary took up nearly a quarter. Nevertheless, the Symphony was a going concern, as indicated by the substantial excess of revenue over outlay.

When Henry von der Heide resigned as conductor in the spring of 1956, possibly for health reasons (he had undergone surgery the previous winter), he left a symphonic orchestra far stronger than the one he had taken charge of six years earlier. The board did not immediately replace him, relying on guest conductors until the summer of 1960. However, the momentum established during von der Heide's tenure assured the Civic Symphony would continue to flourish.

INSTITUTIONAL SUPPORT

The Boise Civic Symphony's reliance on institutional support was typical of most musical groups during the early postwar period. Most relied on the sponsorship of an established organization: the *Elks* Gleemen, the *Kiwanis* Boys Choir, the *Mormon*aires and so on. A group could survive without such sponsorship, as evidenced by the Madrigal Club, but sponsorship certainly remained the norm. Even when financial backing was not an issue, any ambitious program almost always required friendly cooperation from governmental or large-scale nonprofit organizations. Take Music Week, for example. Although it commonly had only a tiny budget, its performances could not have occurred without the assistance of the city, which closed streets for the very popular Fiesta Night (*figure* 67), and the school district,

Fig. 68: Massed pianos in concert, c. 1950s (ISHS)

which allowed presentation of the annual School Night (*figure* 66).

The availability of institutional support could literally make or break even something as seemingly innocuous as children's choirs. A poignant example is the contrast between the Boys in Blue and the Wesley Boys Choir. In early 1950, the Garden City Community Christian Center organized the Boys in Blue: 40 boys enrolled at Whittier School. They took their name from the fact that, lacking funds for choir robes, the boys all dressed in denim. The Boys in Blue appeared briefly, then disappeared. On the other hand, the Wesley Boys Choir, composed of 32 boys in the 4th to 6th grades, began singing as one of the six choirs organized in 1952 by the First Methodist Church. They had choir robes, as well as the dedicated attention of the church's full-time minister of music, and their choir lasted for decades. Sweetness of sound and dedication of the singers had very little to do with the differing fates of the Boys in Blue and the Wesley Boys Choir. Institutional support, rather than musical talent, made all of the difference—not only for those two boys' choirs, but for many other groups then and since.

CONSERVATIVE INNOVATION

The innovative spirit during the early postwar years tended to be conservative. When the First Methodist Church created several age-graded children's choirs, it was certainly innovative: No Boise church had ever previously attempted such a thing. However, those choirs were not meant to explore new kinds of music. Quite the contrary. The Wesley Boys Choir and the others founded in 1952 aimed to help preserve the church's religious heritage. In a similar vein, local music teachers strove to introduce new ways to attract audiences for their students' recitals, that most hide-

bound of all concert forms both aesthetically and socially. The students still had to learn and perform traditionally sanctioned music, but there could be innovations in the recital format. Piano teachers assembled a dozen or more pianos in a large gymnasium (*figure* 68) on which a group of students played for what they hoped would be a crowd of listeners. On another occasion, Bernice Brusen dressed her students in period costumes (*figure* 70) for dramatic effect.

Fig. 69: Mary Bratt with her harpsichord, c. 1950s. (Bratt)

Sometimes, the innovation retrieved a neglected portion of the musical past. In March 1951, the Boise Civic Symphony celebrated the acquisition of the area's first English horn (actually a lengthened clarinet in appearance, with a double reed) with feature articles in the local press and, later, a special concert selection with an English horn solo. In 1957, Mary (Mrs. C. Griffith) Bratt imported the first harpsichord to the Boise Valley—custom-made in Germany for her. She played it at

numerous occasions, wearing a period gown (*figure* 69).

By the last years of the 1950s, however, a fundamentally different kind of innovation came to the fore. "Everything's Up to Date in Kansas City," as the song went in "Oklahoma!",

Fig. 70: Bernice Brusen's students' recital, c 1950s. (ISHS)

and Boiseans had a hankering to move beyond the old and locally accustomed ways and get their music up to date. Consequently, the 1960s soon developed in ways far different from those symbolized by "Bach to Boogie."

6

Fig. 71: "Oklahoma!" program cover (detail), Music Week, 1959. (ISHS)

"Oklahoma!"

"Oh, What a Beautiful Mornin"

The 1960s seemed full of promise for Boise, a time when its leaders might well

have adopted that memorable lyric from "Oklahoma!" as their theme song. In

April 1959, the city elected Robert Day as mayor — a man who had lamented

the town "appears to outsiders as 'Sleepy Hollow.'" He aimed to change

that by launching Boise into a growth mode, doubling the city's area and

population within six years.

Growth continued virtually uninterrupted for the next 40 years, transforming Boise into a metropolis with half of the state's population living within commute distance of the Capitol.

Boise's music leaders shared this vision. Tired of the pokey old, small-town amateurism so characteristic of the preceding era, they looked forward to a new time marked by a level of professionalism that could be favorably compared with the best to be found anywhere in the nation.

Unlike the physical spread of the city, however, musical development in Boise failed to maintain a steady growth. Although the musical scene did ultimately gain metropolitan stature, its growth followed a path filled with twists and turns quite different from the area's population growth pattern. By the end of the 1960s, several music leaders as well as many organizations had disappeared. Those remaining pursued much more modest goals into the 1970s and beyond.

Music Week Reborn

On May 13, 1959, Music Week began a new life with the opening night of "Oklahoma!" (*figures* 71, 72). Few Boiseans had ever seen a live production of a Broadway musical. (Caldwell High School performed the very first in the Boise Valley in 1958, with "Brigadoon.") This innovation delighted everyone. A

Fig. 72: Program cover, Music Week, 1959. (ISHS)

Statesman editorial assured its readers the show was produced on a "more ambitious scale than ever before." In a rave review of "Oklahoma!" running two full columns, Betty Penson concluded "this was Music Week's finest hour."

That was exactly the kind of reaction sought by the Music Week board. For years it had been pondering how to

breathe new life into its annual festival. In 1957, James Bransen told the board "the town has no enthusiasm for it.... No one except parents of the performers comes out to see it." Depressingly enough, that report came four years after the board had concluded it needed "greater showmanship" and "fewer nights of concert-type programs." A growing consensus argued that times had changed, and Music Week programming had to respond with fundamental alterations if it hoped to survive. Consequently, when the board decided in September 1958 that "production of a popular musical is the answer to Music Week's future," this was far more than simply reviving a main event that had been missing for several years. In contrast to the 1920s, when Music Week aimed to build community spirit, now it sought to match the competition posed by television and the movies. The focus of attention turned away from local needs and interests to the national entertainment scene.

Initially, Music Week leaders attempted to soften the blow to the pride of the local performing groups that had previously made up the core of the programs. The leaders promised several choral groups, including the Gleemen and the Choristers, they would each have a special role in the performance, with selected choruses reserved for them to sing. One can readily imagine what a logistical nightmare that could turn out to be. After "Oklahoma!", the choral groups were shunted aside in favor of auditioning for the choruses as well as the leads and supporting roles in the annual musical. Individual talent was all that counted in the new order. Proof of "community involvement" became a matter of counting the large number of people participating in producing the musical. Everyone else served only as members of a passive audience.

There turned out to be plenty of talented local performers, but the question of what play they should perform remained a perennial issue. "Oklahoma!" had been unique in perfectly fitting prevailing local tastes and values. Short of redoing it each year, like a secular version of Handel's

"Messiah"—an option never given serious consideration—the preferred alternative followed the national proclivity for the new, improved

JUNE "JULIE"   EARLE BOYES "JAKE"   "MAGNOLIA" ROSEMARY HILL   DARRELL BADBITT "WINDY"   BETH HOGA

Fig. 73: "Showboat" cast, Music Week 1968. (Schmitz)

annual model. For unexplained reasons, the Music Week board also chose to select a new director for each year's performance, even though Kenneth Hartzler had distinguished himself as the director of "Oklahoma!", and his immediate successor produced a dud.

Consequently, throughout the 1960s Music Week's annual show strove for originality by offering something unlike what had been seen in earlier years.

Keith Patterson selected "Damn Yankees" for the 1960 musical, he explained, to give the community a cross-section of great musicals as a contrast to "Oklahoma!"

The result certainly made a sharp contrast, one that the *Statesman* discreetly chose to leave unreviewed.

Unflustered, the board reiterated its commitment to an annual musical. According to board president Evelyn Donnell, the success of "Oklahoma!" had "firmly established" a new course for Music Week "geared to better meet the changing times." For 1961, the board offered up six alternatives, three Broadway musicals and three older comic operas, asking the public to make the selection. "The Student Prince" gained a very thin plurality, with 26 percent of the vote, while "Annie Get Your Gun" and "Call Me Madame" tied for second at 21 percent. The resulting show pleased its audiences, but the board never repeated the election process.

A wide variety of Music Week shows appeared during the next four years. For 1962, Jacques Brourman (who had come to town the previous year to conduct the Philharmonic) directed "Die Fledermaus," a Viennese opera. Then came "Carousel" in 1963, "My Fair Lady" in 1964, and Henry von der Heide directing "The Merry Widow" (figures 74 and 75) in 1965, using a modernized version first produced in Los Angeles in 1961.

Music Week made one final attempt at what it billed as a return to "the original concept," although in an arch manner totally alien to the attitudes of Eugene Farner and the first leaders of Music Week. The "new look" for

Fig. 74: Sandor Klein as Gypsy Violinist, "The Merry Widow," Music Week, 1965. (ISHS)

Fig. 75: Program cover, Music Week, 1965. (ISHS)

1967 dispensed with *any* musical play. "Like spring fashions," the *Statesman* explained, "it has returned to an old-fashioned theme with a very 'mod' treatment." In place of a musical, "Variety 66" staged a show vaguely reminiscent of "Bach to Boogie." Gib Hochstrasser's Men in Blue provided the big band sound, and Lloyd Carlton's dancers performed extracts from "Swan Lake" accompanied by the Boise Philharmonic. Although apparently well received by the audiences, "Variety 66" offered no pattern for future years. The 1967 program lacked any "mod treatment" and ended up as a clutch of sideshows without any main event.

Evidently, Music Week had passed a point of no return, and the board returned to reliance on a musical play as its centerpiece. In 1968, it picked "Showboat" (*figure* 73) because, according to Gordon Eichmann, it was a "beloved classical musical play," but it also had the attraction of "currently enjoying a tremendous revival" with

the San Francisco Opera launching an extended run in October 1967. Eichmann and Lloyd Carlton went to have a look and returned "enthralled," as Eichmann put it. National models would continue to dominate Music Week programming in the years to come, but it remained to be seen whether they would meet the needs and expectations of local audiences.

THE FIRST YEARS OF THE PHILHARMONIC

When compared with the full-scale rebirth of Music Week, beginning with "Oklahoma!", changing the name of Boise's orchestra in July1960 from the Civic Symphony to the Philharmonic might seem inconsequential. Even hiring Jacques Brourman (*figure* 78) as the first full-time conductor did not prove the orchestra was beginning a new life. However, Brourman lost no time showing that he intended the Philharmonic to have a future far different from what might have been under the old regime. Two weeks after he first rehearsed the orchestra, he asked the board's approval to dismiss five of the musicians and "bring in from

Portland or Salt Lake two car loads of outstanding musicians for the premier concert." The board agreed with this draconian move, merely stipulating that the cost should not exceed $1,000. Considering the fact that the orchestra's total revenue the previous season had only been $6,843, leaving a deficit of $2,100, the board's approval of Brourman's request signified its commitment to major change. If that required more money, so be it. In July 1960, not only did it change the orchestra's name and hire a director; it also announced plans to launch the Philharmonic season with its first Champagne Ball (*figure* 77), limiting attendance to 150 couples. Growth would be in social significance as well as in musical performance.

The changes in July 1960 resulted from a lengthy gestation period matching that of Music Week.

In both cases, the choice pitted community service against aesthetic excellence. During the four years following von der Heide's resignation, the board had reflected on the merits of remaining a community orchestra. However, after inconclusive discussions with Boise Junior College regarding a possible merger with its orchestra, the Civic Symphony board concluded it had no choice but to move forward. It formulated a mission statement, circulated in 1961, which remained relevant throughout the next half-century:

"THE BOISE PHILHARMONIC MAKES BOISE THE MUSIC CAPITAL OF IDAHO AND THE REGION. If we are to enjoy the kind of growth in business and population that has made Boise, we must provide a social climate that inspires development and makes Idaho the BEST place to live and do business."

The board chose well when it hired Brourman to implement its new sense of mission. Although still a young man, he had already accrued an impressive background, serving as acting director of the New Orleans Symphony in 1960. Asked why he would leave New Orleans

Fig. 77: Champagne Ball guests, 1960. (Statesman/BSU)

"The Music Man" is the story of a fast-talking traveling salesman who cannot read music or play any instrument, but who sells the boys of River City a brass band and gorgeous uniforms. His motives are dishonest. But during the weeks he is tricking the customers, he transforms a stubborn, naive town into a singing and dancing community.

From his boyhood memories, Meredith Willson has sentimentally created a fine example of an American Musical based on an American Theme. Willson has said, "I didn't have to make anything up for The Music Man. All I had to do was remember."

The Music Man, produced and directed by Kenneth E. Hartzler, is the fourth musical presented by Musical Productions, Inc. The past shows have been South Pacific, Annie Get Your Gun, and The King and I. Rehearsals will begin soon for the second show of the 1962-63 season, Jerome Kern's "Show Boat."

KENNETH E. HARTZLER
Producer - Director

Fig. 76: Musical Productions, Inc., Kenneth Hartzler and board, with show photos, program for "The Music Man," 1962. (Neil)

for Boise, he replied that conductors had an instinct to "pioneer a cultural renaissance in a community which does not have a full complement of cultural art." Pioneering entails rough work, and Brourman proved himself tough enough to meet the challenge—even if some of his musicians found him a cruel taskmaster.

The Philharmonic during Brourman's years attempted to dominate Boise's musical scene. The game plan, as Brourman saw it, did not focus on musical innovation; the repertoire remained much the same as von der Heide had left it. Rather, Brourman sought multi-dimensional concerts that awed the audience by sheer musical power. That kind of performance began in April 1962 with Orff's "Carmina Burana," the orchestra assisted by the Kiwanis Boys Choir and College of Idaho Choir. The 1962/63 season concluded with the orchestra at the new Cathedral of the Rockies and David Wehr at the pipe organ. The next season began with an opera, "Madame Butterfly," performed in full costume and sets. In the spring of 1964, a performance of Beethoven's 9th Symphony included a combined choir from the three area colleges. Brourman preferred absorbing other organizations rather than cooperating with them. In 1964, he oversaw what turned out to be a temporary merger of the College of Idaho orchestra with the Philharmonic. He produced an annual opera without making any attempt to resuscitate the Boise Opera Company. In 1966, he organized the Philharmonic Chorus, which first sang with the orchestra in December, performing Berlioz' "Childhood of Christ."

Fig. 78: Jacques Brourman (Philharmonic)

For a time, the board fully supported the path being set by Brourman. In March 1963, Paul Ennis declared "the Philharmonic Orchestra is the backbone of many major community efforts in the field of music and indirectly assists in almost every other musical function." In early 1965, a board committee reopened discussions with Boise Junior College about the possibility of merging its orchestra with the Philharmonic. Unlike the case 10 years before, when the College had the upper hand financially, this time the board expected the Philharmonic would control the merged orchestras. Foreseeing a rapid expansion after BJC become a four-year institution, the College board eventually rejected the proposed merger.

Brourman resigned in early 1967. Although his differences with the board remained unpublished, his departure had been "precipitated by a number of things," according to the board's minutes, "including limitations placed on him in terms of bringing violinists from out of town." The board certainly had cause to worry about money. On the bright side, revenues for the 1966/67 season totaled $34,394—about five times what they had been when Brourman arrived. On the other hand, as with most American orchestras, the Philharmonic's proceeds from memberships and sale of season tickets left a large gap between income and expenses. Corporate support helped, of course. For example, its $9,000 note at the bank in August 1963 was secured by Intermountain Gas, Boise Cascade Corporation and the Statesman

Printing Company. Nevertheless, the board felt obligated to do whatever it could to cover its deficits, and fundraising is almost always a stressful business. For example, a concert by Liberace in May 1962 showed a profit of $2,568, but that of Peter Nero in 1966 resulted in a net loss of $418.

In any case, financial concerns were not fundamental. The Philharmonic has, over the past 50 years, proven itself capable of massively increasing its annual revenues. However, neither in the 1960s nor at any time since could the Philharmonic dominate the musical scene in the Boise Valley. The area had too many strong personalities and competing institutions for the Philharmonic to build the kind of musical empire envisioned by Brourman. When the board recognized that reality, it needed a leader with different priorities than Brourman's.

MUSICAL PRODUCTIONS, INC.

While the Philharmonic developed over decades, other Boise musical organizations emerged for a time and then vanished. None had a more meteoric life than Musical Productions. Created by Kenneth Hartzler (*figure* 76) in 1960, it staged nine Broadway musicals, beginning with "South Pacific" (1961) and ending with "Hello, Dolly!" (1970). All were great successes, gaining full houses and rave reviews. But then the company disappeared for the simplest of reasons: Musical Productions depended entirely on the skills and drive of one man, and his retirement drew the final curtain on its plays.

Hartzler had come to Boise in 1937 to teach at Boise High School, but he did not reach his full maturity as a producer and director until 1959, with "Oklahoma!" When Music Week's board appointed Keith Patterson to direct the following year's play, Hartzler went off on his own, creating Musical Productions as his production company. His board included many prominent people, including former Gov.

Fig. 79: Program cover, 1962. (Neil)

Len Jordan as the first board president, but Hartzler was always the dominant force in the company.

He was the epitome of the micro-manager, retaining total control of every aspect of each production. That didn't suit some local talent, who took no part in his musicals, but for others, Hartzler was a pied piper whom they would follow wherever he chose to lead. He double-cast all of his productions, so each had over 100 singers and dancers. Yet the casts always included a cadre of "Hartzler people." "Camelot" (1965), for example, had 26 performers who had sung for him as high school students in the late 1930s.

The results of Hartzler's attention to detail could be seen in every one of his productions. "South Pacific" had 27 different scenes, each changed with very brief "black outs," yet they were done with such speed and precision the audience scarcely noticed. "The Music Man" (*figure* 79) focused on a boys' band, but Hartzler's stage management masked the fact that the band's celebrated "Seventy-Six Trombones" actually amounted to far fewer. Meanwhile, the "great big beautiful Hartzlerian chorus" proved to be the star of the show, according to Betty Penson's *Statesman* review.

Hartzler's retirement after "Hello, Dolly!" left a permanent, unfillable hole in Boise's musical leadership. However, his skills as producer and director had raised the bar on musical comedies with local talent that other directors would ignore at their peril.

MUSIC FROM THE CATHEDRAL

What would it be like if Hartzler's style of showmanship shaped a church's music program? David Wehr (*figure* 80) provided an answer at the Cathedral of the Rockies (the name taken by the First Methodist Church when it occupied its new structure in 1960.) Wehr was very much the showman, while also being an outstanding musician. He had much in common with C. Griffith Bratt. He could play recitals for the American

Guild of Organists, and he rehearsed his choir for six months before it performed the Northwest premier of Bernstein's "Chichester Psalms" in February 1967. Yet there was an immense difference between them, demonstrated by the fact

Fig. 80: *Gordon Eichmann, Nancy Wehr, Doris Downum, David Wehr, 1966. (Panko)*

that Wehr and his wife, Nancy, sang solos in Hartzler's production of "The Music Man," a dabbling with the charms of Broadway unimaginable for Griffith and Mary Bratt.

Initially Wehr attempted to resurrect a mass chorus drawn from several church choirs, but his Symphonic Choral Society fared no better than had Bratt's Boise Civic Chorus in the late 1940s. First announced in January 1959, the Society gave a couple of concerts and then disappeared in 1961.

However, the Cathedral of the Rockies had enough musical resources of its own to serve Wehr's purposes. Its nine or 10 choirs had been presenting a Festival of Christmas Music since 1952 (a tradition continuing today as Christmas at the Cathedral) and could be readily adapted to other eye-catching productions, such as "Prophet Unwilling." This oratorio, with music by Wehr and libretto by Herbert Richards (the senior pastor at the Cathedral) was unveiled in March 1962. "Not massive in terms of such old works as Handel's 'Messiah'," according to a review in the *Statesman*, but "it was presented with great dramatic impact."

The greatest dramatic impact achieved during Wehr's tenure came from the Cathedral Bell Choir, a group of about 20 high school students Wehr organized soon after his arrival in 1958. Beginning in 1962, the Bell Choir took a series of tours that gained it an international reputation. They began with the Seattle World's Fair on May 28, 1962, followed in June 1964 with an appearance at the New York World's Fair, including a video taping for later broadcast. Wehr was also invited to give a concert on the Fair's carillon. In June 1965, the Bell Choir gave a concert at Disneyland. The capstone came in 1967 with an invitation to perform at the U.S. exhibit in Montreal, Canada, at Expo '67. Who knows what might have followed if Wehr had stayed in Boise, but in the spring of 1968 he resigned to take a teaching position in Florida at the University of Miami. The Cathedral of the Rockies continued an active music program, but without Wehr's distinctive flamboyance. That left the challenge of performing to a national audience to other Boise institutions.

generated a storm of disapproval, not only from Borah boosters but also from community leaders. "Their light must not be hidden under any bushel,"

trips set a precedent for other out-of-state performances. Those sometimes involved trips to distant cities, such as Boise High's band and drill team

Fig. 81: Massed high school bands at Bronco Stadium, c. 1960s. (von der Heide)

PLAYING FOR A NATIONAL AUDIENCE

Boise's high schools didn't wait for David Wehr's departure to begin their own out-of-state programs. They started the same way as the Cathedral Bell Choir: performing at the Seattle World's Fair in the summer of 1962. The Boise school board initially vetoed the invitation for the Borah High School band to play in Seattle. That

the *Statesman* editorialized. "Here is opportunity and it should be accepted with enthusiasm." Failure to perform in Seattle would give Boise a "black eye," according to Jeff Roberts, chairman of the Chamber of Commerce Industrial Development Committee. "We should get our feet wet. This community should grow up." Grudgingly, the school board finally approved the trip. Of course, as a matter of equity, that led to the Boise High School band also going. And, just as the board had feared, the Seattle

performing in October 1966 during half-time at the 49ers/Raiders football game in San Francisco. Alternatively, the performance could be taped, such as Borah High's choir concert in December 1962, for nationwide radio broadcast on NBC.

Whatever doubts the school board had about such developments, Henry von der Heide surely must have enjoyed them. Although now the head of Boise schools' music programs, which kept him away from the podium most of the time, he clearly relished heading up the annual performance of massed bands in Bronco Stadium (*figure* 81) at the Boise/ Borah football game or Veterans' Day observances. Such performances strongly suggest that von der Heide, as well as the thousands in attendance, had an eye cocked for the possibility of network TV coverage. The shows delighted many Boiseans, but wouldn't it be grand if it also led to national coverage?

Where might it all end? The limit was apparently reached in December 1972, when the Borah band requested approval to attend an international music festival in Brussels, Belgium. The school board, doubting the boosters could raise the $96,000 needed for that trip, denied the request, and the lack of widespread protest indicated the community generally agreed with the decision. However, in July 1973, Gov. Cecil Andrus announced he had designated a group of 24 singers from Boise-area high school choirs as Idaho's Singing Ambassadors to Europe. Furthermore, in April 1973, the Capital High School band and drill team had marched in the national capital's Cherry Blossom Festival parade, with the drill team winning first place among the many participating drill teams. Boise's schools have continued playing for national audiences into the 21st century.

INTO THE SHADOWS

While the high school bands marched off to national attention, many of Boise's singing groups slipped off into the shadows. By the end of the 1960s, some had utterly disappeared, including the Mormonaires and the Elks Gleemen. Others, such as the Kiwanis Boys Choir, sang publically only once every few years. Even the Choristers and the Madrigal Club, which managed to survive into the 21st century, sharply reduced the number of their public appearances. Where they had performed several times a year in the 1950s, they now offered no more than an annual concert—and sometimes not even that. Only one new group appeared, the Showtimers in 1963, but they were quite different from the others. Unlike groups such as the Gleemen and the Madrigal Club, which relied on the pleasures of good fellowship to hold them together, the Showtimers was made up entirely of singers such as Bert Burda, Gordon Eichmann and Stanton Stringfellow who were all well-known soloists in their own right. And even the Showtimers lasted only a few years beyond the demise of the Gleemen.

This negative trend went unnoticed in the local press, and its causes remain unexplained. Possibly it reflected the changing times, when a common popular culture shared by most of the community was being replaced by an increasingly diversified society   made up of groups that had less and less in common with one another. The changing times split up the kind of audiences the singing groups relied upon. Take, for example, "Dry Bones," the Negro spiritual that the Gleemen made a great local hit, rendered in black light. In a time of Freedom Marches and the assassination of the Rev. Dr. Martin Luther King, Jr., the Gleemen's light-hearted presentation might have seemed to some in the audience as being in questionable taste, possibly even racist. By 1968, Boiseans were being forced to confront such issues, and that had a great effect on the city's musical life.

Fig. 82: Pete Seeger album cover, 1966. (Internet)

Pete Seeger Comes to Town

SUNDAY AFTERNOON IN THE PARK

On Oct. 6, 1968, Pete Seeger gave a concert at the band shell in Julia Davis Park,

singing to an audience numbering about 3,000. Local media hailed the event "A

Victory for Reason Over Fear," to quote the title of a Statesman editorial. His

invitation by the students of Boise State College (now BSU) had provoked such an

outcry from political conservatives that the college president vetoed the concert.

chapter

7

However, the college's governing board decided in favor of the students, although the concert was discretely relocated from the college mall to the park across the Boise River. Sheriff Paul Bright had assured a rally opposing the concert that he had documented proof Seeger was a Communist. Seeger certainly had a notable record of social activism, but he looked and acted in such a comfortable down-home way (*figure* 83) that it was hard to think of him as a dangerous public enemy. He told a local reporter, "If I do my job right, even people who came to boo will see these songs as an attempt at building an America that I—that we all—want." The songs he sang in Boise, opening with "Old Joe Clark" and including "Good Night Irene" and "The Lion Is Sleeping," seemed innocent enough. Even when he offered some of his own protest songs, such as "Where Have All the Flowers Gone," only the most hidebound opponents could find them to be subversive.

Nevertheless, Pete Seeger's concert in Boise, for all of its unthreatening tone, marked a fundamental turning point in local sensibilities. Boiseans could no longer live as though they remained in the placid 1950s. Hippies and the drop-out culture of San Francisco's Haight-Ashbury had appeared remote and unrelated to their own life. When Dan O'Leary attempted a "love-in" on the Capitol steps in August 1967, only one other person joined him, and O'Leary conceded Boise "just isn't ready

Fig. 83: Pete Seeger, Julia Davis Park band shell, 1968. (Statesman/BSU Library)

for hippies yet." However, the racial strife and violence of 1968, marked by the assassinations of Dr. Martin Luther King Jr. in April and Robert Kennedy in June, were accompanied by musical reverberations that might be muted in Boise but could not be ignored. The full significance of Seeger's concert lay in the fact that the students had invited him rather than a much more aggressively counter-cultural musician or group who would have delighted in "freaking out the squares" with music and lifestyle akin to that portrayed in Tom Wolfe's "Electric Kool-Aid Acid Test." Boise could not hide from the music and cultural politics of the time, but was far more comfortable receiving them gently from folk singer Pete Seeger instead of the outrageous Ken Kesey and his Merry Pranksters, as described by Wolfe.

Even better, Pete Seeger could be seen as something like a much more famous older brother of Boise's own most successful folk singer, Rosalie Sorrels (*figure* 84). Both had gotten their start collecting regional ballads and traditional folk music, he in the South in the 1930s, she in Utah and Idaho in the later 1950s. Both had gradually moved into social protest music characterized by a sympathy for the weakest members of society and a belief in the dignity of every human being. By the time Seeger came to Boise in 1968, he and Sorrels had become good friends, and they later performed in concerts together.

Stanton and Nancy Stringfellow's daughter Rosalie grew up in Boise, graduating from Boise High School in 1951. Soon thereafter, she married and moved with her husband to Salt Lake City. Although Sorrels did not finally resettle in her home town until the 1980s, she made frequent trips to Boise and, beginning in mid-1967, she stayed with her mother for several months at a time. She first began to gain a national reputation in 1966, when she was invited to perform at the Newport Folk Festival. By that time, she had four albums to her credit (a number that had increased to 20 by 2005.) Rosalie Sorrels has always been fondly regarded in Boise. The *Statesman* ran a lengthy profile in 1979 entitled "Notorious stranger returns to Boise," but judging from the content of that article, her notoriety resulted primarily from her having been too much of a stranger for too long. Whether

Fig. 84: Rosalie Sorrels, 1967. (Ronayne)

she sang lullabies or anti-war songs, she was accepted by Boiseans as one of their own. She successfully bridged the gap between young people with social concerns and their conservative elders — at a College of Idaho homecoming concert less than a week

Fig. 85: Buffalo Springfield, c. 1960s. (Internet)

after Pete Seeger's Boise appearance and for decades thereafter.

SLOW TO ROCK

1968 was also the year when socially conscious rock 'n' roll music artists first made it to Boise, with Buffalo Springfield (*figure* 85) performing at Capital High School Auditorium

on March 22. The group had a soft, harmonious sound later known as folk rock, but its lyrics sometimes had political or cultural overtones. Its best remembered song, "For What It's Worth," written by Stephen Stills and first released as a single in January 1967, opened with . . .

There's something happening here
What it is ain't exactly clear . . .

and repeatedly warned

Stop, children, what's that sound
Everybody look what's going down.

It wasn't clear that those in the audience took heed of the warning; the *Statesman* reviewer claimed "nobody just walked out of that auditorium .... They were dancing, skipping, finger-snapping, singing."

Of course, as commentators had been saying ever since the mid-1950s, rock could be culturally transformative in its music, regardless of the lyrics. In effect, Elvis Presley challenged the standing order when he swiveled his hips. On the other hand, rock could be rendered socially innocuous and become what critics dismissed as "bubble gum music," and that's what happened in Boise until near the end of the 1960s. Only a small handful of nationally known rockers came to town, and they could be viewed as little more than curious novelty acts. Fats Domino and Jerry Lee Lewis both appeared at the Miramar in July 1961, but neither Domino's Rhythm & Blues, as heard in his 1955 hit, "Ain't It a Shame," nor Lewis' Country & Western sound typified by his "Great Balls of Fire," troubled local leaders. The Beach Boys appeared in September 1964, but who could be worried about the cultural overtones of a group lauding "Surfin' USA?"

By the mid-1960s, Boise had a number of rock groups. One that persisted, off and on, to this day is The Mystics (figures 86,87), fronted by Tim Woodward. Most were ignored by the media, even when one group gained national attention with its hit records.

Figs. 86,87: The Mystics before (1963) and after (1965) the British Invasion. (pnwbands.com) Figs. 88,89 (below): Paul Revere & the Raiders, 1960s. (Internet)

That was Paul Revere and the Raiders, the most famous rock group to originate in the Boise area. Organized in 1957, they were already advertised as "recording artists" when they played the Blue Note Club in Garden City in December 1960. Five years later, they had million-selling hits and toured nationally. Nevertheless, not until September 1969 did they have

a major concert in Boise—at Bronco Stadium with the Beach Boys. Whether they imitated the clean-cut appearance of the Beach Boys (figure 88) or later donned their 18th-century costumes (figure 89), they received very little recognition from their home town. As Revere ruefully noted to Statesman writer Tim Woodward in 1977, "You know, I get the feeling that people around here never really knew how big we were." They were all too easily forgotten. Their music could be dismissed as run-of-the-mill. Their biggest protest song, "Indian Reservation," didn't come out until 1971. It affirmed . . .

*Though I wear a shirt and tie
I'm still part redman deep inside.*

While that might raise some eyebrows in Boise, it failed to provoke any significant controversy.

Boise's cultural leaders faced no fundamental challenge from rock 'n' roll until 1972. That's when Alice Cooper did its blatantly obvious anti-establishment thing in a concert at Firebird Raceway, midway between Boise and Emmett.

WHERE TO PLAY?

Pushing Alice Cooper so far away from downtown Boise may have been intended to minimize its impact. That location also pointed up Boise's critical lack of concert venues, made even worse when the Miramar burned down in May 1967 and the Columbian Club closed its clubhouse in 1970. The auditoria at Boise and Capital high schools provided the only large indoor concert halls until the opening of the Boise State University Pavilion (now known as Taco Bell Arena) in 1982 and the Morrison Center in 1984. Occasionally, the high schools could serve for rock concerts. "Godspell" (November 1974) and "Jesus Christ Superstar" (April 1981) both played at Boise High's auditorium. However, its limited seating provided inadequate revenue for expensive touring groups. The Julia Davis Park band shell served local groups (*figure* 90), but there was no way to charge admission in the park. Boise State's gymnasium could hold

about 4,000, and a number of nationally known groups did perform there, including Steppenwolf (March 1971), The Byrds (January 1973) and Ike and Tina Turner (May 1973). Unfortunately, the authorities took a jaundiced view of

any further rock concerts. The following year Charlie Daniels seemed "strong on rock and light on bluegrass," and the city fire marshal closed the gym to *all* concerts. Not until 1981 would that prohibition be lifted.

Fig. 90: Rock concert, Julia Davis Park band shell, 1976 (Statesman/BSU)

audience behavior at the gym. After an Edgar Winter concert in September 1975, college officials declared "the security just wasn't good enough" and banned

Consequently, concerts by expensive entertainers, both rock groups and pop stars such as Kenny Rogers, had to perform outside at Bronco Stadium or in buildings at the Fairgrounds, which had neither air conditioning nor comfortable seats. Whether or not a sufficiently large local audience existed to justify construction of a really big concert hall continued to be debated throughout the 1970s. On the one hand, promoters repeatedly declared that they needed a venue seating at least 10,000 to justify bringing in top talent. In 1979, Boiseans were aghast at the news that Fleetwood Mac had been booked in Pocatello. "Why," the *Statesman* asked, "would a super group start its world tour in Pocatello"? The answer lay in the venue: the Minidome, seating 11,800. Could Boise justify building a facility equally large? Doubters could point to erratic attendance figures to make their case. In 1974, Frank Zappa drew only 900 at the Fairgrounds, far less than the 5,000 hoped for. In 1977, Carole King played Bronco Stadium to barely half a house, with only 5,000 of the 9,700 seats occupied, even though the tickets cost only $5 apiece.

The flood of sold-out concerts at the BSU Pavilion definitively ended that debate, but attendance figures for grandstand entertainment at the annual Fair could have been taken as clear signs that "if you build it, they will come." Nationally famous musicians had been appearing for decades at Nampa's Snake River Stampede, but the Western Idaho State Fair did not follow suit until 1973. The Jaycees, which sponsored the music that year, suffered a reportedly "big loss." Undaunted, in 1974 they booked Paul Revere and the Raiders, a mariachi band, and a number of other musicians. Attendance figures grew rapidly thereafter. In 1977, Flash Cadillac and the Continental Kids (a group specializing in 1950s style rock) had 7,500 at its early show and 9,500 at the later one. The very next night, Country & Western star Mel Tillis drew

Fig. 91: Rick Nelson, 1979. (Statesman/ BSU Library)

10,000 at the 7 p.m. show and 12,000 at 9:30 p.m. In 1979, Rick Nelson (*figure* 91) sang to 12,000. Granted, the audience got free admission to the grandstand shows, after paying only $3 for admission into the fairgrounds, so it remained unclear how many would pay just to hear the musicians. Nevertheless, the numbers undeniably showed a large potential audience for name groups playing in a comfortable indoor facility, such as the BSU Pavilion when it opened. Meanwhile, thousands turned out for traditional parades, regardless of the weather. The 1970 Fairyland Parade, for example, included 31 drill teams and 22 bands with more than 3,000 participants.

The shortage of spaces for smaller audiences was somewhat mitigated in early 1976 when Boise State opened its 435-seat Special Events Center. Much more important, however, were the great number of spaces previously little-used for musical events, places as diverse as the YWCA auditorium, the Open Door coffee house on Broadway and even the Idaho Outdoor Association hall on Brazil Street in a residential neighborhood near the airport. The IOA hall provided space for Idaho Folklore Society programs, one of a variety of sponsoring organizations that first appeared in this period. The Boise Gallery of Art probably presented more programs than any other new sponsor, with its Museum After Hours concerts featuring groups as diverse as Boise State faculty ensembles, Ragged But Right (a local bluegrass band), an early-music group from Seattle called Western Wynde Consort and the Boise Banjo Band. The Boise Gallery of Art also provided new concert opportunities at its annual fundraising craft show, Art in the Park. Paradoxically, the shortage of concert venues resulted in an almost endless variety of new types of concerts: silent movies accompanied

Fig. 92: Providence, "Sense the Dawn" album cover, 1971. (Tompkins)

by the restored Ada (now Egyptian) Theater organ; a fundraising sing-a-long staged by the Borah High School choir at Shakey's pizza parlor; a Christmas concert in the Capitol Rotunda by the Treasure Valley Tuba Association; bluegrass house concerts with the address advertised so that interested persons could drop in and listen. These and many others demonstrated the liveliness of the Boise musical scene, which thrived regardless of the shortage of conventional concert venues.

PROVIDENCE

The most intriguing Boise rock band that formed in the 1970s, Providence epitomized the fluidity and creativity of the local musical scene. At first glance it might look like a typical rock band (*figure* 92; front cover lower right), but the instrumentation was

anything but typical: cello, viola and harpsichord but no drums (an almost unthinkable omission for a rock band). Organized by Bart Bishop in 1970, four of its six musicians were recent high school graduates, yet half of the band had already played with the Boise Philharmonic. Nor did the musicians share the rebellious opposition to prevailing cultural values so commonly found among rock groups. They told a *Statesman* reporter they had been most influenced by Jesus Christ, William Wordsworth and Mahatma Gandhi. Jim Cockey joined Providence after hearing the group at St. Michael's Cathedral. Although Providence had a sound strongly reminiscent of the Moody Blues, they played only music that the members had composed.

Soon after Bishop and the other members of Providence moved to Portland, they met the Moody Blues. After hearing their demo tapes, the Moodies invited Providence to England to cut their first album, released as "Sense the Dawn." This remarkable turn of events caught the attention of the Boise media, and Providence enjoyed a very good local press. Nevertheless, the group lasted less than three years before disbanding. Tom and Tim Tompkins and Jim Cockey went back to England to tour with Moodies' Justin Hayward and John Lodge as the Blue Jays (*figure* 93), and that ended the performance history of Providence.

Providence had but a fleeting existence and issued only a single album, but it served as a launching pad

Fig. 93: Tom Tompkins (top), Jim Cockey and Tim Tompkins. rehearsing in London, England, 1976. (Tompkins)

for the musical careers of several of its musicians. Bart Bishop went on to form other rock groups, while Tom Tompkins and Jim Cockey developed careers in the world of classical music. Since 1985, Tompkins has been principal violist with the Boise Philharmonic. Cockey moved to McCall, where he founded a chamber orchestra and established himself as a composer. The Boise Philharmonic commissioned and performed his First Symphony in 1993. Rarely has a short-lived rock band had such a fruitful and diversified impact on the music of its time.

THE PHILHARMONIC COMES OF AGE

The Boise Philharmonic reached maturity during the 1970s. It began the decade as an orchestra with promise but remained less than fully developed. The *Statesman* review of a concert in December 1967 typified that status. The reviewer termed the choice of program "well made" but conceded the orchestra "is not the Philadelphia." Still, "they are fine musicians, and they performed well." The Philharmonic, in short,

pleased the home town folks but did not yet measure up to national standards. By June 1980, on the other hand, it made its first visit to a larger city, performing in Salt Lake City's Mormon Tabernacle. Two years thereafter, the internationally respected Tabernacle Choir acknowledged the Philharmonic's stature as something of a peer by paying it $6,200 to accompany the choir at the dedication of BSU's Pavilion.

This maturation came in two stages, roughly matching the tenure of the two conductors during those years. Mathys Abas (*figure* 94) replaced Brourman in the summer of 1967. Abas' heavy Dutch accent reminded Boiseans of his highly romantic background. He had fought the Nazis in his homeland during World War II, was captured and then escaped from a train bound for a German concentration camp. Avoiding any equivalent excitement in Boise, Abas stabilized the Philharmonic's local standing by reaching out to all potential audiences. He defended the value of pops concerts. "I don't see anything wrong with 'Rhapsody in Blue,' a couple of arias, something light so they won't have to work so hard, the audience or the orchestra." He frequently offered lecture/demonstrations to enhance understanding of concert selections. Beginning in the fall of 1968, he added a Preview Night (the night prior to the first concert) to give people a chance to see how a rehearsal went. That same season he also added children's concerts, with an abbreviated program accompanied by commentary to assist youngsters' enjoyment of the music. Very infrequently, Abas challenged his listeners with difficult, unfamiliar performances, such as Honegger's "Symphonie Liturgique" in February 1970. Most of the repertoire, however, was limited to Beethoven, Brahms and other familiar 19th century classics. By the end of his first season, the *Statesman* reported "Philharmonic Establishes Artistic Progress."

Abas graciously assisted the board and Auxiliary in their unending struggle to generate additional revenue since, under the best circumstances, ticket sales left a significant gap between expenses and income. The 1968 Champagne

Fig. 94: Mathys Abas, c. 1968. (Statesman/BSU Library)

Ball typified the combination of social and aesthetic stylishness favored by the Philharmonic's fundraisers in this period. The elegant dinner/dance included Mary Bratt playing her harpsichord and an ensemble accompanying Lloyd Carlton's interpretive dancers' rendering of "Winter" from Vivaldi's "Four Seasons."

On the other hand, financial growth was not Abas's strong suit. The Philharmonic's annual budget did grow during Abas's tenure, but only at a rather modest pace. The 1967/68 financial statement showed income at $39,141 and expenses totaling $34,222. The financial statement for 1972/73 showed income at $59,700. When Abas resigned in the spring of 1973, he concluded "we've seen progress in many

Fig. 95: Daniel Stern, 1977. (Statesman/BSU Library)

ways" but "we've come to a point where it's time to part ways." The frustratingly slow growth in the Philharmonic's budget surely played a major part in occasioning Abas's departure.

Daniel Stern (*figure* 95), appointed in May 1974 to replace Abas, was cut from quite different cloth. Having earned his doctorate from the University of Oregon in music education, Stern surely shared his predecessor's interest in community outreach. For example, Stern played an instrumental role in the founding and subsequent support of the Treasure Valley Youth Symphony. Nevertheless, he focused most of his energies on the rapid growth of the orchestra, both musically and financially.

One month after his appointment, he told the Philharmonic's Executive Committee he "would like to develop a cycle of music for one, two or possibly three years." The Executive Committee genially replied by affirming the conductor's programming prerogative. However, it soon turned out that Stern's desire to explore what he called the "fringe"—music composed before 1790, unfamiliar 19th century pieces and anything written in the 20th century—provoked board fears that such adventurous programming would reduce season ticket sales. This tug and pull in programming resulted in concerts primarily made up of standard works spiced with those from the "fringe." The April 1976 concert can be taken as fairly typical of programming during the early years of Stern's tenure. The orchestra performed four works that spring evening, of which three were "standards" and one came from the "fringe." It opened with Beethoven's "Prometheus Overture," followed by Rachmaninoff's "Piano Concerto No. 3." Prior to ending the evening with Berlioz's "Romeo Alone," however, Stern challenged his audience with the very complex 3rd (or "Camp Meeting") Symphony of Charles Ives. On a few occasions, Stern dumped such cautious programming and presented a lengthy work that impressed the audience with his audacity, even if they found it hard to enjoy. In March 1980, the Philharmonic performed Ernest Bloch's "Sacred Service" (the Jewish equivalent of a Catholic mass) assisted by three choral groups singing in the original Hebrew. Stern's eclectic and somewhat pragmatic programming succeeded in keeping the support of the unadventurous while significantly broadening the Philharmonic's repertoire.

Stern's programming philosophy may have worried some board members, but they must have been delighted with his aggressive approach to financial growth of the Philharmonic. In sharp contrast to Abas's record, Stern's leadership produced a remarkable growth in revenues. The increase during Abas's six years amounted to 53 percent; Stern's first eight years yielded an increase exceeding 400 percent! This not only met the board's desire for institutional growth, but effectively responded to heavy pressure from the Idaho Commission on the Arts, a crucial source of funds for the Philharmonic. In March 1979, Carl Petrick, the Commission's executive director, spoke to the Executive Committee. He issued a number of dicta, including a budgetary goal of $200,000 by 1982. The Philharmonic met that challenge with room to spare. The treasurer's report in August 1982 showed income of $240,302, with a deficit of $15,235. The following year, income had leaped to $325,651, with the deficit reduced to $3,608. Thereafter, the Philharmonic never looked back; revenues continued to grow each year.

To achieve such rapid financial growth, the Philharmonic had to pull out all of the stops.

Traditional sources of revenues—season ticket sales, corporate sponsorships and Auxiliary (later Guild) functions such as the Champagne Ball—all had to be made even more productive. In addition, new sources had to be found. The most profitable were special concerts by famous entertainers. If they were also artistically notable, such as Itzak Perlman, all the better. But neither Stern nor his board caviled at more commercial attractions. They booked Doc Severinsen in November 1979, entailing a fee of $10,000. The budget for the Pops concert in May 1981 totaled $22,346 and resulted in a profit of $4,300. These numbers may not seem all that large from a latter-day perspective, but it should be remembered that a decade or so previously the total annual budget for the Philharmonic had amounted to less than $40,000. Of course, that had been a time when no one could be sure that the Philharmonic was here to stay. By the early 1980s, its permanence had been conclusively established.

OPERA REVIVED

The 1970s turned out to be not only a fine time for the Philharmonic, but a decade that saw the organization and development of two other major local music groups. What is now Opera Idaho began as the Boise Opera Workshop in September 1970, while the Boise Master Chorale originated in February 1975.

So many years had passed since opera's heyday in Boise that almost no memory remained of that distant time. Typically, Jon Enloe, a director with the Boise Civic Opera, told a reporter in 1980, "opera is the new art form. It's almost like America discovering art for the first time." Consequently, the Philharmonic board

Fig. 96: "The Ballad of Baby Doe" in rehearsal, 1980. (Statesman/BSU Library)

proved highly dubious when Mathys Abas asked in January 1969 whether he should schedule an opera. It concluded "we should not tackle an opera as we do not have the people in Boise to undertake it." Actually, as Daniel Stern declared in the fall of 1977 as he prepared "La Traviata" (figure 98), "we have a very high professional caliber of performers with this particular cast." In fact, he went on to say, "we have all of the ingredients necessary for a great opera." Sharing that belief, about 30 people had met in 1970 to organize the Opera Workshop. They immediately selected Abas and Gordon Eichmann to direct its first production, "Cavelliera Rusticana," a late 19th century Italian opera. That performance was

Fig. 97: Program cover, 1972. (Bratt)

well received, and what became known as the Boise Civic Opera in 1973 continued to mount one or two productions a year.

Why opera could succeed in Boise remained an open question. Some observers attributed its success to a large number of people moving to town from larger cities, but that failed to explain the great popularity of "The Ballad of Baby Doe" (figure 96) in Horseshoe Bend and Idaho City when the Civic Opera toured it in the spring of 1980. It is certainly true that opera is the most complex musical form, one requiring a deep pool of talent and money to be successful. Evidently, as Stern testified, there was sufficient talent in Boise, occasionally supplemented by imported soloists and directors. As for the money, that never came easily for any arts organization, but in Boise, opera had the invaluable support of Esther Simplot, wife of Idaho's richest man and a talented singer in her own right. She joined the Civic Opera board in early 1975. The following year she sang a leading role in Mozart's "Cosi Fan Tutte." The list of corporate donors reached far beyond the Simplots. When planning the October 1972 premiere of "Rachel (*figure* 97)," Griffith Bratt's second opera, the Philharmonic board anticipated a shortfall in revenues of $1,850 and lined up the Idaho First National Bank and Intermountain Gas to underwrite the losses. In fact, to the surprise of many, "Rachel" ended its two-night run with a surplus of about $1,700, mute testimony that opera had very wide support in Boise.

But what kind of opera should the local company perform?

Fig. 98: "La Traviata," 1977. (Statesman/BSU Library)

It took nearly a decade to answer that question. It originally proposed, according to Hazel Weston (Bratt's librettist), to present grand opera in both modern and classic traditions. Hence, "Cavelliera Rusticana" was soon followed by "Rachel." But there were problems with that goal. Classic operas were usually in a language other than English, while modern ones could be musically challenging: That for "Rachel," according to Abas, who conducted it, "is very, very tough." Perhaps the Civic Opera ought to present "Bits and Pieces" — selections from several different operas, which it did in March 1975 and occasionally thereafter — but that sacrificed the integrity of a full opera. Ultimately, the Boise opera company settled on the classics, sometimes sung in English, and generally avoided the musical and thematic challenges of modern works. Indicative of this approach was its call in April 1980 for auditions, naming four operas planned for the following three years: "Madame Butterfly," "Cosi Fan Tutti," "The Year of the One Reed" (Bratt's latest, focusing on Montezuma and pre-Columbian Mexico), and Menotti's "The Old Maid and the Thief." The first two ended up being performed, with the modern works quietly pushed aside. Such cautious programming, like that in the early years of the Philharmonic, may have been necessary to assure institutional survival.

BOISE MASTER CHORALE

Wayne Richmond, minister of music at Cathedral of the Rockies, formed the Master Chorale in the spring of 1975. Unlike the Civic Opera, the Chorale immediately settled into a very simple program, one that might well have been adopted by the Civic Festival Chorus 50 years earlier: a Christmas concert — usually Handel's "Messiah" — and an oratorio on a religious theme in the spring.

Neither Richmond nor his successor, Charles Fisher, who took over in August 1979, showed any signs of chafing at the Chorale's playing, in effect, second fiddle to the Philharmonic. Even though "Messiah" is essentially a choral work, and the Master Chorale had more than 100 voices while the Philharmonic supplied only a couple dozen instrumentalists, Stern rather than Richmond conducted the Christmas concert for the first two years. In future years, the Chorale would greatly broaden its repertoire, but during the first decade it never wandered beyond the bounds it had originally set for itself.

Fig. 99 Collage: Master Chorale, Boise Philharmonic Orchestra perform "The Messiah," St. John's Cathedral, 1975. (Statesman/BSU Library)

Consequently, it had a rather curious status as a musical organization. On one hand, the public obviously enjoyed the return of the traditional Christmas performance of "Messiah," which had not been heard in Boise since 1960 until the Master Chorale's 1975 presentation (figure 99), and filled St. John's Cathedral for both performances. On the other hand, however, the public spotlight rarely focused on the Chorale. Thus, the *Statesman* review of the March 1977 concert, the first that Richmond conducted, gave

almost no space to the Chorale. The following year the review, entitled "Boise Philharmonic shows proficiency in Verdi's 'Requiem,'" failed even to mention the Chorale. Given that kind of press, it was symbolically appropriate for the Chorale to merge with the Philharmonic, which it did in the fall of 2011.

JAZZING WITH GENE

Gene Harris (*figure* 100) is a perfect example of the unpredictability of historic events. No one in 1975 could have predicted that a black world-class jazz pianist would move to Boise and settle here for the remainder of his life. And yet that's exactly what happened in 1977, when the 43-year old Gene Harris decided to retire in Boise. He had no longtime connections with Boise; he was born and raised in Michigan and developed his career in the Midwest. Nevertheless, Harris quickly and comfortably fit into Boise's music life.

His widespread fame greatly flattered Boise's pride. During his career, he issued far more albums than any other Boisean. By the time he died in 2000, his discography included 61 entries with him as lead artist and another 40 where he was a contributing artist. Yet he always took a very open, unassuming stance toward anyone who showed an interest in jamming with him, whether it be Lt. Gov. (later Gov.) Phil Batt or a musical instrument repairman from Glenns Ferry. As he explained in 1979, "they know I'm not Gene Harris, the guy who's made records, and you're just Boise musicians. They know I'm Gene Harris, a Boise musician that's made records."

Gene Harris had a profound impact on Boise's concert life, as we will note in subsequent chapters, which started when he abandoned his "retirement" within a year of his arrival. His Tuesday evening jam sessions in the lobby of the Idanha Hotel almost immediately became a notable event for musicians and local jazz lovers. In September 1978, he played during the cocktail hour for the dinner dance celebrating the 25th anniversary of the Philharmonic Auxiliary. In October 1980, he opened the Caldwell Fine Arts season (Caldwell's equivalent of Community Concerts). In following years he managed to combine world tours with casual jazzing in Boise without any apparent effort, always the smiling, relaxed entertainer who just happened to be one of America's greatest jazz pianists.

Fig. 100: Gene Harris, Idanha Hotel Lounge, 1982. (Statesman/BSU Library)

Reaching for the Big Time

By the end of the 1970s, many Boiseans had become increasingly frustrated

by their inability to enjoy live performances by the nation's top musical

talent. The area had attained sufficient population and affluence to afford

the most expensive musicians, but Boise had no place for them to perform.

Within a few years that all changed.

The Boise State University Pavilion, now known as Taco Bell Arena (opened in 1982) and the Morrison Center (opened in 1984) allowed Boise to join the big time in musical performances, fundamentally and permanently changing the city's musical life.

THE ONE THAT GOT AWAY

The Morrison Center for the Performing Arts as it exists today differs in many ways from the one originally conceived by the Harry Morrison Foundation. Announced in January 1972 by Velma Morrison, Harry's widow, as a "legacy of his will," it was intended to provide a first-class concert hall in a dramatic setting. As designed by Boise architect Glenn Cline, it would have had a monumental presence, almost like a temple of the performing arts (*figure* 101). Ann Morrison Park, opened to the public in May 1959, included space for such a facility immediately east of the reflecting pool and fountain, but prior to Harry's death in July 1971 nothing had been done

to fill that space. Nor did Boise hasten to accept Velma's proffered gift. In July 1973, eighteen months after it had been made, *Statesman* writer Tim Woodward lamented, "the offer has met with delay, fund problems, and apathy."

By November, inflation in construction costs combined with declines in the value of Morrison-Knudsen stock (the basis of the

Fig. 101: Artist's concept, Morrison Center, c. 1975. (BSU Library)

Foundation's gift) meant that construction of the Morrison Center would require several million dollars in addition to the Foundation's gift. Following another 18 months of delays, community leaders formed a committee to get the Morrison Center built. Chaired by Ralph Comstock, president of

First Security Bank, and including Joe Albertson, founder of the supermarket chain bearing his name, among its members, the committee persuaded the Boise City Council to set a November 1975 bond election for $5.1 million. Despite zealous efforts by the committee and many arts supporters to overcome worries about tax consequences and fears that the Morrison Center might blight the park's appearance, the vote fell short of gaining the two-thirds majority required for bond measures. Voters favored the bond issue 16,092 to 8,812, but that missed the required super-majority by 2 percent. Unwilling to believe the city would really reject the Morrison Center, its supporters decided to go for another bond election in May 1976, staging a "low key" campaign along with a drive to garner $500,000 in pledges from local donors. The second election, however, ended all hopes for a Morrison Center funded by Boise taxpayers. The favorable vote declined to a margin of only 54 percent to 46 percent. The Morrison Center would have to be entirely reconceived if it were to become a reality. As it turned out, more than 13 years would elapse between the original announcement of the gift and the opening of the Morrison Center.

THE PAVILION

While the Morrison Foundation and local arts supporters struggled to find a way to build the Morrison Center, Boise State University planned and built its Pavilion with remarkably little fuss or difficulty. It took less than five and a half years to get the job done. Finding the money to pay the construction costs, totaling $17.5 million, proved to be no problem. Almost everyone agreed BSU needed such a facility. It had jumped into an era of very rapid growth, progressing from a junior college to a four-year institution in 1965, becoming Boise State College in 1968, and gaining university status in 1974. Total enrollment shot up, increasing by 73 percent between 1970 and 1980. BSU needed a place for university-wide functions, such as graduation, and total enrollment by 1980 was twice the capacity of the existing gymnasium. Students, eager for adequate room for the burgeoning basketball program as well as for concerts, agreed to a fee of $50 per semester. Proceeds from those fees plus a contribution of $5 million from the Bronco Athletic Association assured the state's Permanent Building Fund Council that bonds for the construction would be paid in timely fashion,

Fig. 102: *Boise State University Pavilion (interior, exterior), 1982 (Statesman/BSU Library)*

and it approved the construction contract in September 1979. The Pavilion was completed on schedule, in time for graduation ceremonies in May 1982 to inaugurate its use.

The design of the Pavilion was unblushingly functional. Although you could find some architectural elegance if you looked just right (*figure* 102), the architect (Glenn Cline, who had designed the original Morrison Center) devoted his skills as a designer primarily to maximize the arena's ability to serve a wide variety of uses. Budget concerns threatened to cut the seating capacity to less than 10,000, but Cline managed to find ways to provide seating for 11,245 (*figure* 102). The arena occupied less than half of the Pavilion's total area of 200,000 square feet. The remaining space served a number of functions important for the university, but public attention has always focused on the arena.

What exactly the Pavilion arena would be used for remained to be seen. Dexter King, appointed Pavilion manager in April 1981, conceded "we really don't know what the market is." At its opening the *Statesman* declared "a new era of entertainment and sports will begin in Boise." Both were right. Management had to feel its way into programming strategies, but the result served a remarkably wide range of public functions. Following the commencement ceremony, the Pavilion provided space for a boxing match on closed circuit TV on June 11, concert by Kris Kristofferson on July 1 and a week-long Billy Graham crusade in August attended by 101,550. By mid-July, the *Statesman* thought it already evident, as it titled an editorial, "Boise breaks into the big time."

The "big time" turned out to be a wide variety of popular music and only rarely anything of a serious aesthetic character. Boise State scheduled the Mormon Tabernacle Choir, accompanied by the Boise Philharmonic, to perform on September 24 in observance of the 50th anniversary of the school's founding. However, even with a very modest ticket price of only $5 (less than half of the usual cost for most popular concerts), only 8,000 attended—appreciably fewer than for many of the other 26 concerts in the Pavilion for the year ending in July 1983. The definitely passé Beach Boys had attracted more than 10,000 on July 9, and Heart (a rock band of limited national repute) drew 9,000 on July 17. When Boiseans

had a chance to hear a current national star such as Kenny Rogers, whose "The Gambler" had topped all of the charts the previous year, they responded with locally

Fig. 103: Wayne Newton (above) and Willie Nelson perform at BSU Pavilion, 1983. (Statesman/BSU)

Fig. 104: Fans in line for Kenny Rogers concert, 1982. (Statesman/BSU Library)

unprecedented enthusiasm. More than 1,500 people stood in line to buy tickets (*figure* 104), and the September 12 show had a Standing Room Only audience. Equally full houses enjoyed Barry Manilow on Oct. 8, Wayne Newton on April 17 and Willy Nelson on July 15 (*figure* 103). Not only were these much bigger "names" than Boise had previously been able to attract, they also appeared two or three times more frequently than the pace of major shows prior to the opening of the Pavilion. Rock 'n' roll had its place on the schedules, but Country & Western and mainstream pop stars such as Manilow clearly outnumbered the rock bands and generally drew larger audiences.

In sharp contrast to the kind of dour distrust that had led to closing the BSU gymnasium to concerts for several years, the managers of the Pavilion evinced a broad tolerance for fans who actively enjoyed their music. For example, the *Statesman*'s report on the March 12 performance of the Oak Ridge Boys, attended by 10,000, began "it had all of the earmarks of a foot-stomping, knee-clapping tent meeting ...." Such behavior might have led to the re-closing of the gymnasium, but the authorities at the Pavilion showed no inclination to come down hard on people for simply having a very good time.

Pavilion rental policies showed a comparable readiness to include as broad a range of activities as possible. Unlike the situation later faced by the Morrison Center, with repeated complaints that stiff rental fees shut out local groups, the Pavilion charged non-profit groups as little as $1,500. Consequently, for example, the Central Assembly Christian Life Center could afford to present a Christmas cantata on December 23 and 25, 1983, with free admission.

Within the first year or so, the Pavilion had formulated programming policies that it followed for many years thereafter. George Manning, the administrative services manager, summarized those policies in a 1990 interview: "Although we are controlled to some degree by what shows are available, we still try to be diverse; we still try to bring in a good mix of shows."

Fig. 105: Velma Morrison in front of the Morrison Center, 1984. (Statesman/BSU Library)

Asked for his definition of " a good mix," Manning replied, "country and western, rock 'n' roll, and family shows... . We have to monitor what's healthy, what's wholesome." As an example of what that would be excluded, he mentioned "O, Calcutta," which had just been banned by the school district from performing at Boise High School Auditorium because of its blatant display of nudity.

With such minimal restrictions, generous rental rates and locally unmatched space, the Pavilion single-handedly revolutionized Boise's popular concert life. Never again would Boiseans be embarrassed by major performers playing Pocatello but skipping Boise.

THE MORRISON CENTER RECONCEIVED

The crucial if rarely recognized fact about the Morrison Center is that its construction resulted from successful financial planning that avoided clearly expressing priorities for its use. One might almost say that the avoidance was necessary, that pulling together the complex funding package would have been an impossible task if the Morrison Foundation and Boise State leaders had attempted publically to reconcile the competing hopes and dreams of the various interests that joined together to get the Center built. Local arts groups expected it to enhance their performances. The *Statesman* spoke for many civic boosters when it welcomed the original announcement of the Morrison Foundation gift: "This project would greatly enhance the city's role as a center of cultural activity in the West." When Velma Morrison (*figure* 105) made that announcement, she had noted that Harry had always been particularly fond of Broadway musicals and had hoped Boise would have a place for them to be properly presented. Boise State expected the Center to magnify its music department's programs. What if one or more of those motives, all of them laudable in their own way, conflicted in the actual operation of the Center? That question never received serious public attention, which focused instead on questions of location and funding.

It took three years to settle on the location. Various alternatives got some attention, including the Fairgrounds and downtown, as part of what eventually became the Center on the Grove convention center. Ultimately, the Boise State campus was chosen. In June 1979, the Morrison Foundation gave Boise State $3.5 million for a performing arts center. Initially, it was intended to replace the music building near the Liberal Arts Building, but within a few months its present site was selected on the northwest edge of campus near the Boise River.

Before construction could begin, of course, funding had to be lined up. Once again, the cost skyrocketed, threatening to replicate the situation in the early 1970s. At first, it was thought the Morrison Center could be built on the BSU site for about $5 million to $6 million, with the state matching the Morrison Foundation gift. Soon, however, Ernest Lombard, the architect, revised the estimate sharply upward to more than $11 million. In fact, the eventual tab roughly matched that of the Pavilion, at more than $17 million.

The state did approve $2.5 million for the project, but that left a very large gap to be filled by private donations. In an outstanding example of local support, the donations *did* come in, beginning with $1 million from Jack Simplot, who said, "This thing has been kicking around for eight or ten years. It looked like if it didn't get a shot in the arm, it would fizzle again." Other corporate leaders followed suit: $100,000 each from Boise-Cascade, First Security Bank, Idaho First National Bank, H.J. Heinz and William and Gladys Langroise. Morrison-Knudsen added $150,000. By January 1981, small donations totaled $340,000. To complete the funding package, in October 1981 the Morrison Foundation added another $3

Fig. 106: Morrison Center, academic entrance. (Internet)

Fig. 107: Morrison Center, Main Hall, 1982.
(Statesman/BSU Library)

million to its original commitment. In June, 1981 the Permanent Building Fund Council approved the Morrison Center plan, and construction finally began in the fall.

The exterior appearance of the Mor-

Fig. 108: James Ogle rehearsing Boise Philharmonic, 1992.
(Statesman/BSU Library)

rison Center (*figure* 106) did not please everyone. It seemed "rather boxy," as state Sen. Richard High put it when he saw preliminary designs in August 1980. Lombard retorted, "I don't believe Mr. High understands the project." Unlike Glenn Cline's design for the Ann Morrison Park project, it lacked an overall sculptural presence that Senator High missed but which Lombard dismissed as irrelevant. Leading a tour of the partially completed structure in May 1983, Lombard called it a "very functional building," a work of "pure form." That may have gone a bit far, but in Lombard's eyes the exterior massing clearly reflected the fact that the Morrison Center contained a wide variety of spaces, in-

cluding not only the Main Hall, which most people focused on, but also a number of smaller rehearsal and performance spaces, as well as offices and classrooms for BSU's large music department. The tallest "box" (in the center of the photo, *figure* 106) enclosed a very commodious fly gallery, which would play a crucial role in accommodating shows requiring numerous and complicated set changes.

The interior, on the other hand, delighted both performers and audiences. The Main Hall (*figure* 107) with 2,000 seats, all of them enjoying good sight lines, had a spacious stage and superb acoustics that could be "tuned" for various kinds of productions. It also had a dazzling, multi-story foyer perfect for the social art of "seeing and being seen."

Opening night on April 7, 1984, was a gala, black-tie affair, "a truly grand opening," gushed the *Statesman*. Evidently those attending did have a grand time, but there were ominous implications of problems that would hound the Morrison Center for years to come. In the first place, opening with

"My Fair Lady" evinced nothing like the grand touch of the world-famous Mormon Tabernacle Choir, which the Pavilion had invited to solemnize its opening. Although this production of "My Fair Lady" used a local cast, it was produced and directed by Fred Norman, the Center's executive director. Finally, pricing the tickets at only $8 and $12 missed a golden opportunity to generate funds for a facility with a budget that would be chronically running in the red.

All three of these factors signaled a programming policy that would prevail during the Center's first years, a policy of extreme caution both aesthetically and financially. It had been evident well before its opening that most local groups would be unable to pay the high rental fees without help. Velma Morrison started an endowment fund with $2.5 million to be matched by local donors, a challenge ful-

ly met by November 1989. Nevertheless, only the Boise Philharmonic could regularly generate the full houses necessary to afford performing in the Main Hall. That gave the Philharmonic the full benefit of the new concert venue. James Ogle (*figure* 108) has said he came to Boise in 1987 to replace Daniel Stern as conductor primarily because of the full houses

Fig. 109 "Cats," 1991. (Statesman/BSU Library)

and the outstanding acoustic qualities of Morrison Center. For other local groups, however, the Main Hall usually was unaffordable. Music Week did not perform there until 1988, and only then because

of a special dispensation by Mrs. Morrison. The Boise Opera Company could only afford the Main Hall by performing the most well-known (and therefore the least artistically adventurous) operas, such as "Car-

Fig. 110: Fred Norman (Statesman/BSU Library)

men," which immediately followed "My Fair Lady" and "Madame Butterfly" in February 1985. Soon the Opera Company found it better to perform at less expensive venues. The only "local" productions other than the Philharmonic regularly using the Main Hall were school groups sponsored by BSU's music department, such as a high school orchestra festival in December 1984 and the Idaho Choral Festival in February 1985, which boasted seven high school choirs and BSU's Meistersingers.

Most of the performances staged in the Main Hall were utterly "safe," unimaginative, and scarcely lucrative, such as the lively but innocuous Up With People, the Count Basie Orchestra (which gained an audience of only 1,000), and Myron Floren, the popular accordionist with Lawrence Welk. The first series of musicals began in September 1984 with "Seven Brides for Seven Brothers." This programming reflected the tastes of Mrs. Morrison (*figure* 105) and Fred Norman (*figure* 110), her right-hand man and the Center's executive director from 1982 to 1989. Evidence of that duo's control of Morrison Center programming came in late 1985 with 19 performances of "Camelot," directed by Norman and presented free of charge as a regal gesture by Mrs. Morrison. Obviously "Camelot" was popular, with a total attendance of 43,000, but no one explained how it fit with the financial needs of the Center.

Not until 1991 did the Main Hall host a production responding to its full potential and generating a really large revenue. That came with "Cats," which had eight performances between October 31 and November 5 (*figure* 109). No other house within 300 miles could accommodate this very ambitious Broadway show. It required five semi-trucks to haul its sets, which took more than a day to install. The promoter said he needed 9,000 seats sold to break even. Boiseans very quickly demonstrated their willingness to step up and be counted, buying 7,000 tickets at $33-40 the first day of sale. The full run of 12,000 sold within three days, leading to the addition of two additional shows, which also sold out. Reviewers raved over the production. "It's like a dream," declared Bill Roberts in the *Statesman*. "Don't question it. Enjoy it. ... 'Cats' is captivating."

Once every year or two thereafter, the Main Hall displayed equivalent road-show blockbusters, such as "Les Miserables" and "Miss Saigon." Eventually, local groups would also, if infrequently, rise to the heights made possible by the Main Hall, such as "The Nutcracker" by Ballet Idaho. Nevertheless, the Main Hall continued to be, for the most part, more of a potential than a demonstration that Boise had entered the big time.

RECITAL HALL

When people refer to concerts at the Morrison Center, they usually are thinking about the Main Hall. Perhaps Carolyn Terteling and her committee, planning the first month's activities celebrating the opening of the Morrison Center, thought of the Recital Hall (*figure* 111) as just another instructional space like the band room. In any case, they passed over it without a single public bow to its exquisite character. Its only publically noted concert in the spring of 1984 was a Suzuki violin recital on May 5. Not until the following autumn did the Recital Hall begin to be regularly used.

Tucked away in the middle of the Morrison Center without any ceremonial entrance comparable to the Main Hall's foyer, and seating only 180, the Recital Hall could easily be overlooked. However, it proved to be ideal for musicians seeking a place for intimate concerts. So much attention had been lavished on its design and construction in order to perfect its acoustics that the contractor called it "the million dollar room."

Use of the Recital Hall has never been an issue. Unlike the Main Hall, no one has ever publically complained that its rents were too high. Although it has only rarely been used for amplified music, it stands ready to accommodate a very wide variety of instrumental ensembles and vocal groups acoustic such as the Choristers. Many of the Recital Hall concerts have been quite esoteric, unlikely to attract a large audience. Take, for example, "Poetry and Music" on Nov. 8, 1984, featuring James Hopper on clarinet, George Thomason on guitar and several poets reading their work. Or "Percussion and Opera' on December 3, with the BSU percussion ensemble and Opera Theater. Lovers of chamber music very quickly organized a series, beginning in November, 1984, that led to the founding of the Boise Chamber Music Society in 1985. Its annual subscription series have long since been sold out each year. Although it originally booked regional trios and quartets, by 1986 it had already begun bringing in nationally known groups such as the New York Baroque Ensemble.

Reaching for the big time has often seemed to be a matter of massive productions, such as Kenny

Rogers and his "space age light show" in the Pavilion and "Cats" in the Main Hall. Nevertheless, a truly first-rate musical center ranks in the big time not only because it entertains thousands, but also because it provides space for excellent performances attracting only a small handful of listeners. That is why the Recital Hall must be included in any account of how Boise became a center

of musical performance. In October 1985, Bela Sike performed in the Recital Hall. A pianist from Hungary and the BSU music department's first artist in residence, Mr. Sike may not have gained much public attention, but he symbolized the importance of the Recital Hall in Boise's music life—an importance that has continued unabated to the very present.

Fig. 111: Recital Hall, Morrison Center, 1984 (Statesman/BSU Library)

Alive After Five

BACK TO THE FUTURE

One might suppose that all of the effort to build large-scale spaces to attract

nationally known performers, what I have called "Reaching for the Big

Time," would cast local, low-budget musical performances so far into the

shadows they would practically disappear from Boise's concert scene.

In fact, quite the opposite happened. In those same years that saw the opening of the Pavilion and Morrison Center, Boise also welcomed growing numbers of free outdoor concerts, renewing and adapting a local tradition dating back to the Columbia Band in 1910 and the beginning of Music Week in 1919.

"AFTERNOON IN THE PARK"

That tradition had never totally disappeared. Boise's Municipal Band had continued to give Sunday afternoon concerts during the summer months at the Bandshell in Julia Davis Park. However, by the 1970s few people had much interest in sitting and listening to a brass band play Sousa marches and selections from well-known orchestral classics. No longer serving any useful purpose, the Municipal Band vanished after the 1984 season. In its place appeared a wide variety of

Fig. 112: Boise Banjo Band, Julia Davis Park, Music Week, 1986. (Statesman/BSU Library)

groups performing all over town.

Appropriately enough, in 1976 Music Week initiated the new way of presenting free open-air concerts. Retrieving what in decades past had been an annual Variety Night, Music Week recast the evening into an "Afternoon in the Park," a daytime event in Ann Morrison Park. All musicians were publically invited to participate, and many responded. The 10 different groups scheduled for Saturday, May 1, ranged from the Gleemen to the Hillside Junior High School Stage Band. The next year offered 12 groups (most of them different from those in the first year), including the El Korah Swing Band, the Happy Harpers (a group of gospel singers) and the Madrigal Club. The music they offered could be as nostalgic as the Boise Banjo Band (*figure* 112) or as

currently trendy as bluegrass by Ragged But Right.

A gradual resurgence of free outdoor concerts occurred during the next few years. The venues were as traditional as the corner of 8th and Idaho with (shades of the Columbia Band) Boise High School's eight-piece brass choir kicking off downtown Christmas festivities, or as new as "Jazz Along the River" on the Boise River bank near

Fig. 113: Dancing to The Mystics, "Streets for People," 1992. (Statesman/BSU Library)

the Morrison Center. Unlike the days when the Municipal Band played in the band shell, one could no longer confidently describe the standards of behavior expected of the audience. Those varied as much as the type of music being performed. Whatever the expected posture while listening to a Salvation Army

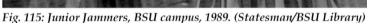
Fig. 115: Junior Jammers, BSU campus, 1989. (Statesman/BSU Library)

Fig. 114: Salvation Army Good Friday concert, 1987. (Statesman/BSU Library)

band (*figure* 114), it certainly differed from dancing in the street in response to a local rock band during a Streets for People celebration (*figure* 113). During its final years, the Municipal Band still performed in Julia Davis Park, but other groups offered something quite different at the Bandshell. Thus Calvary Chapel began in 1983 its "Summer in the Son," a series of contemporary Christian music.

Consequently, in 1985 when the city parks department faced the task of replacing the Municipal Band's summer concerts, it responded to the diversity of prevailing tastes by sponsoring a wide variety of groups at three different locations. In addition to the Bandshell on Wednesday evenings, noontime concerts occurred on Wednesdays at the City Hall plaza on Capitol Boulevard and in C.W. Moore Park at 5th and Grove. During that first summer series, D-ZYN, a rock band, played at the Bandshell, Billy Braun, a popular local Country & Western performer, appeared at Moore Park, and the Junior Jammers (*figure* 115), a children's old-time fiddling group from Nampa, entertained the public at City Hall plaza.

The stage was almost set for Alive After Five. One thing remained to be done: creation of a space in the middle of downtown specifically designed for outdoor festivities that could accommodate thousands of people. That moment came in December 1986 with the dedication of The Grove, south of Eighth and Main streets, a 31,000-square-foot circular plaza with a fountain at its center. Created by the Boise Redevelopment Agency (BRA) at a cost of $573,000 in a desperate, last-ditch effort to rejuvenate a downtown depressingly dominated for a dozen years by several square blocks of empty space, The Grove was an immediate success. It began the permanent reversal of the public's avoidance of the urban renewal area by offering crowd-pleasers such as those at the dedication, which featured music by a calliope and The Yankee Doodle Dandies, a song-and-dance group of children ages 4 to 12.

ALIVE AFTER FIVE

Alive After Five has been around so long, celebrating its 25th anniversary in 2011, that probably few people remember why it began. In 1987, downtown Boise faced the fact that the construction of the Towne Square Mall at the junction of I-84 and I-184 marked the conclusive defeat of the 10-year-long effort to build a covered mall in the center of Boise. Would downtown become another of those pathetic urban places that lived only during business hours? Or could it develop ways to keep the heart of the city flourishing in the evenings? Hence the name of the event, which expressed a hope (long since fulfilled, of course) that downtown Boise could be Alive After Five.

It had a disarmingly simple format: a free concert at The Grove each Wednesday from 5 p.m. to 7 p.m. throughout the summer months, during which people could stroll about and buy food and drink (including beer and wine) from stands on the edge of the plaza, while their children were free to play around and run through the fountain. The BRA, which sponsored the programs, had no grandiose expectations. According to Robert Loughry, its executive director, "it could

be just a brief kind of after-work get-together." Therefore, neither he nor his board expressed dismay when it started out very modestly. Even with Gene Harris kicking off the original program

Fig. 116: Gene Harris, Alive After Five, 1987 (Statesman/BSU Library)

on June 10, 1987, by jazzing (*figure* 116), the audience numbered barely 300. "It's exactly what The Grove was designed for," enthused Loughry. "An active place, a place for people."

Its ambience proved to be the key to Alive After Five's success. Occasionally "name" entertainers such as Gene Harris, Juice Newton or Paul Revere and the Raiders performed, but those tended to be on special occasions such as the annual party thrown by the state lottery.

Such big names attracted very large audiences, totaling 5,000 in September, 1989. However, like all really successful urban plazas, The Grove could be an enjoyable place however small or large the attendance. Only rarely did the programs feature classical music, but attendees could expect to hear a wide variety of popular music, including performances by the Capital City Jazz Band, the Mystics playing rock and roll, Onomatopoeia unveiling Kevin Kirk's jazzy originals, the Chicken Cordon Blues (*figure* 117) and Kathy Miller wailing soul, and the Braun Brothers rendering their version of

Fig. 117: Sandon Mayhew, Chicken Cordon Blues, c 1990s. (Internet)

Country & Western. Once in a while, the local talent reached beyond simply providing a concert. For example, Basque dancers accompanied by their own musicians enlivened the evening on July 27, 1987. Whatever the music being offered, those attending felt free to relax, chat and dance if so inclined. In sharp contrast to the very staid behavior at Municipal Band concerts, where people were expected to observe all of the proprieties—properly dressed and sitting quietly—Alive After Five set a tone that encouraged everyone to "do their own thing" in whatever dress they chose to wear, be it a three-piece suit for a man just leaving his office or shorts and a T-shirt for anyone fortunate enough to be able to change into comfortable garb. (This informality applied to

Fig. 118: Hyde Park Chamber Players, c. 1990s. (Tompkins)

many other free outdoor concerts in the years following, too.) Over time, the casual has tended to be increasingly more in evidence than the formal, but

has never resulted in serious crowd-control problems. Everyone—musicians, members of the audience and those designated to keep the peace—has found it relatively easy to catch the social beat, as it were, with maximum pleasure and minimum hassle.

CATCHING THE BEAT

Alive After Five offered an almost perfect model for bringing an unprecedented variety of music and performers to Boise audiences. The ease, however, with which The Grove sidestepped crowd-control issues left unsettled the question of how to "catch the social beat" in park spaces commodious enough for all sorts of open-air concerts but lacking the panoply of facilities at the Grove. How to serve a wide variety of publics who didn't necessarily share all of the same assumptions about appropriate behavior on such occasions? In some cases, reliance on tradition served to avoid conflicts. Thus, the Boise Philharmonic offered Pops in the Park during the Boise Gallery of Art's annual

Art in the Park, playing a free concert at the Bandshell each September from 1987 to 1991. Apparently a symphonic concert generally evoked attitudes among the

Fig. 119: Curtis Stigers, 1991. (Internet)

audience that kept everything quiet and peaceful. But what about a rock concert, such as the one Curtis Stigers and his new band staged in June 1987? Tom Governale with the Parks Department took strong exception to those who casually littered the grounds and in a few cases urinated in the Rose Garden. He peremptorily banned all further rock concerts scheduled in the park for that summer because "they were not paying the respect needed for the park." The *Statesman* agreed "an ugly precedent such that cannot be ignored."

Fortunately, over the next few months wiser heads developed a compromise heading off what might have turned into an unhappy standoff. By the spring of 1988, Governale found rock performances a "little bit easier to manage" and allowed them back into the park. For their part, the rockers accepted the presence of private security people paid for by the radio stations and other sponsors of the free concerts. Meanwhile, everyone made an effort to behave themselves, having a good time without needlessly provoking their neighbors. The City Council passed various rules limiting the consumption of alcoholic beverages near the concert area, but those rules would have been unenforceable if most of the audience hadn't exercised discretion when bringing a small flask in their pockets.

The net result of this ad hoc emergence of a genial social code governing outdoor concert behavior—what I have called "catching the beat"—was the complete absence of anything remotely akin to Woodstock or similar phenomena. In Boise the cops were cool, the audiences were laid back, and everyone had a good time without significant collateral damage.

NOON TUNES

Free outdoor concerts in Boise have continued to thrive in the 20 years and more since the launching of Alive After Five, providing a remarkable diversity of music and performers for the public to enjoy. Noon Tunes has achieved

Fig. 120: The Trenchcoats, Boise State University Quad, 1993. (Statesman/BSU Library)

some kind of record for sheer variety of musical styles and forms. Begun in the spring of 1989 and still continuing in 2011, Noon Tunes presents programs at noon on Wednesdays on the BSU cam-

pus reflecting the unembarrassed eclecticism of "Bach to Boogie" recast into the casualness and seeming spontaneity of Alive After Five. Sometimes the same groups have performed at both venues, including the Junior Jammers and the Trenchcoats, a rock 'n' roll vocal quartet (figure 120). But Noon Tunes also offered many groups highly unlikely to appear at Alive After Five, ranging all the way from the Hyde Park Chamber Players, an unusual trio of two strings and a bassoon (figure 118) playing classical music, to The Often (a New Age jazz group), Bermuda Triangle (playing rock classics), and the Aspen Jazz Ensemble. Noon Tunes has never received much publicity. It has been and continues to be more like a weekly gathering of street musicians than a formal concert, and in that regard it harkens back to the near anonymity of the Columbia Band in 1910. Of course, the Columbia Band soon evolved into the Boise Municipal Band, while Noon Tunes has shown no tendency to evolve into anything more than what it started out to be: a fun-loving celebration of music, contributing something special to Boise's everyday life.

Boise River Festival

Nothing could be further from the unpretentiousness of Noon Tunes than the Boise River Festival with its gigantic balloon floats, crowds mounting to the tens of thousands and hype redolent of Madison Avenue. In fact, presenting music was almost incidental to the aims of the Festival's founders and planners. Conceived in 1989 and premiered in June 1991 as a way to deal with what some perceived as Boise's "self-image problem," as well as to fill empty springtime hotel rooms, the Festival aimed to create a spectacular array of events attracting thousands of visitors. Tellingly, the *Statesman* headlined its page-one story on June 28,1992, "Day 3: 160,000." There was nothing remarkable about the fact that, as part of the vast array of activities during the week-long Festival, the planners included numerous concerts. Rather predictably, they offered a selection of national celebrities, including Maynard Ferguson, Doc

Severinsen, and Chubby Checker.

Far less predictable, however, was the Festival's inclusion of a full spectrum of local performers. Of course, Gene Harris was one of them, but at the opposite end of the fame spectrum were entertainers such as the band One More Time With Style, composed of several hundred former and current high school and college band members, which formed to participate in the 1993

Fig. 122: Doug Martsch, Built to Spill, c. 1990s. (matusiak.org)

Festival parade. Those in charge of each year's Festival held auditions open to all local musicians, providing them an opportunity to perform on the same day, if not on the same stage, as their nationally known peers. Those selected through auditions included groups that had been on the

Fig. 121: Steve Fulton, House of Hoi Polloi, c. 1990s. (Fulton)

local scene for a number of years, such as Steve Fulton's House of Hot Polloi (*figure* 121), and groups just starting out, including John Nemeth, still a teenager at the time, whose Fat John and the Three Slims wowed the crowds with its hard-driving rendition of the blues. Participating in the Boise River Festival probably served as an important launching pad for Nemeth, but other groups might well have succeeded without the assistance of Festival exposure. For example, Doug Martsch (*figure* 122) and his rock band, Built to Spill, had already started recording by 1994, when they played at the Festival, and their 1995 contract with Warner did not necessarily hinge on their Festival appearance. Nevertheless, the fact remains that the Boise River Festival showed a notable inclusiveness in scheduling music concerts, something Boiseans take for granted but which is by no means typical of every American city. Although the Festival lasted for only a dozen years, by which time mounting debts and waning revenues forced its termination, free outdoor concerts that showcase a wide array of talents and types of music remain a vital part of the music scene in Boise.

10
Here, There, and Everywhere

The location of music performances in the Boise metropolitan area went

through a dramatic change in the 1990s. For most of the 20th century, the

vast majority of concerts occurred in or near downtown Boise. Typically,

soon after Frederic Fleming Beale moved to Caldwell in 1912, he began

commuting to Boise for most of his performances. For the next 70 years, only

rarely did the flow go the other way.

Beale premiered his opera at Boise High School; Bratt's operas premiered in Boise. Not until the 1990s did Boise composers hear their works premiered in Caldwell. With the notable exception of the annual week-long National Oldtime Fiddlers' Festival in Weiser that began in the early 1950s, Boiseans saw little reason to travel beyond Ada County for their musical enjoyment.

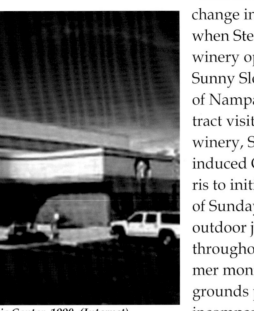

Fig. 123: Nampa Civic Center, 1990. (Internet)

This pattern reflected the paucity of attractive concert venues in Canyon County. Not until 1961, with the opening of the 900-seat Jewett Auditorium on the College of Idaho campus, did Canyon County have a first-class concert hall. While Jewett Auditorium did significantly enrich the musical life of the area, particularly with the Caldwell Fine Arts Series (comparable to Boise's Community Concert series), its audiences probably included very few Boiseans.

That all began to change in 1983, when Ste. Chapelle winery opened on Sunny Slope, south of Nampa. To attract visitors to the winery, Ste. Chapelle induced Gene Harris to initiate a series of Sunday afternoon outdoor jazz concerts throughout the summer months. With its grounds providing incomparable views across the Snake River Valley to the Owyhee Mountains in the distance, Ste. Chapelle offered an attraction unmatched in the Boise area. Over the next few years, a growing number of Boiseans traveled to Ste. Chapelle for jazz as well as blues concerts and a variety of other musical offerings. That set the stage for the emergence of a lively concert life extending beyond downtown Boise to venues throughout the metropolitan area.

NAMPA CIVIC CENTER

During the 1990s, Nampa gained a full range of outstanding concert halls. First came the Nampa Civic Center (*figure* 123), which opened its doors on 3rd St. South in downtown Nampa in January 1990. Its construction costs had already been fully paid on opening day, thanks to 20 years of fundraising efforts by the Majors and Minors, a 50-voice community chorus, and a wide range of other local supporters. James Ogle, director of the Boise Philharmonic, pronounced the 640 seat auditorium "a marvelous facility." Ogle focused on its acoustic qualities, but the most remarkable aspect of the Nampa Civic Center was its commitment to serve the whole community. Rather than following Boise's quest for aesthetic excellence featuring programs of national quality, the Nampa Civic Center gave priority to community groups, stressing accessibility both in terms of repertoire and participation. Thus, the Majors and Minors, founded in 1969 and directed for many years by Helen Hoalst, offered song and dance routines of old-time favorites performed by casts selected without auditions. Similarly, the Music Theatre of Idaho, founded in 1996, stated its purpose as providing "opportunities for individuals to expand and explore their interests in musical theatre production" with "family-oriented, affordable live" performances. That mission statement could have been written by Eugene Farner and the other founders of Boise's Music Week. It expressed attitudes that had long since waned in Boise but remained alive and well in Nampa.

The Nampa Civic Center did not spurn aesthetically ambitious classical music. As soon as it opened, it booked the Boise Philharmonic to perform each of its concerts on the night prior to its Morrison Center presentation, a practice that continued until the opening of the much larger Swayne Auditorium in 1997. The Civic Center also scheduled concerts similar to the Community Concerts series.

However, there was no implied cultural hierarchy in the Civic Center's programming. A 1993 full-page ad in the *Statesman* terming the Center "The Jewel of Treasure Valley" also announced a concert by Bo Diddley. The Center unabashedly celebrated the

rural traditions of Canyon County with performances of the Junior Jammers, children doing oldtime fiddling routines. And then there was an ongoing parade of local groups, such as the Treasure Valley Showtime Chorus, both in the auditorium and, eventually, in the adjoining Calliope Gardens, which by 2000 offered "Fun in the Sun," a series similar to Alive After Five. If this all seemed like musical hash to critical connoisseurs it, sounded like community responsiveness to many people in Nampa and the surrounding area whose patronage rendered the Nampa Civic Center an ongoing success.

LANGROISE TRIO

While Nampa initiated a musical tradition with its Civic Center, the College of Idaho in Caldwell launched a remarkable renewal of a tradition begun by F. F. Beale 60 years earlier, a tradition combining high-quality classical performances on the campus with full participation in Boise's concert life. Thanks to the great generosity of a

Boise benefactor, this renewal came with a level of financial support unimaginable in Beale's time.

In May 1991, the College of Idaho formally accepted a gift of $2 million from Gladys Langroise to endow a resident string trio at the College,

Fig. 124: Langroise Trio, College of Idaho. (C of I)

with the violinist also serving as concertmaster of the Boise Philharmonic and the other two trio members also taking principal roles with the Philharmonic. This combination of roles had been conceived in conversations between James Ogle, director of the Philharmonic, and Robert Hendren, president of the College. Ogle recalls that they presented the idea to Mrs. Langoise over lunch at the Arid Club, and she immediately agreed to underwrite it. Subsequently, she also gave an additional $6 million to build Langroise Hall to house the College's fine arts programs and include a recital hall similar in size and acoustic quality to the Morrison Center Recital Hall.

The Langroise Trio (*figure* 124) began life fully endowed—the first musical group in the Boise area to enjoy such patronage—and with a contractual mandate to participate as leaders in the Boise area's musical life. It has been singularly successful in meeting that rather complex mandate. Selection of the trio came slowly. Samuel Smith on cello came first, then David Johnson on viola a year later. Finally, the appointment in 1997 of Geoffrey Trabichoff as violinist (replacing Susan Demetris-Dundon) completed the present trio. In addition to their teaching duties and participation in Boise Philharmonic programs, the trio offers several concerts a year, both in Langroise Hall (where admission is always free) and in Boise (usually at the Esther Simplot Performing Arts Academy). In addition, the trio accepts invitations to play elsewhere in the area, ranging from

Fig. 125: Esther Simplot Performing Arts Academy, 1996. (Internet)

the Caldwell Fine Arts Series in Jewett Auditorium to a brown-bag lunch at the Egyptian Theater in Boise and the Nazarene church in Mountain Home. Although it usually performs as a trio, occasionally it includes one or two guest artists. The trio's repertoire is notable for its breadth, including standard works by Beethoven and Brahms, early music by Henry Purcell, and also new work it commissions from local composers, including David Alan Earnest of Nampa and Jim Cockey of Boise.

Lovers of classical music sometimes express the fear that rock 'n' roll has swamped good music. Of course, there is no question that audiences at popular music venues dwarf those attending a Langroise Trio program. Nevertheless, for prospects of longevity, the trio far surpasses any and all pop groups.

ESTHER SIMPLOT PERFORMING ARTS ACADEMY

Downtown Boise gained during these same years a new music institution even more important than the Nampa Civic Center and the Langroise Trio. Modest and unassuming as its exterior appearance might be (*figure* 125), the Esther Simplot Performing Arts Academy offered invaluable support for classical music in the Boise area by providing rent-free space for the Boise Philharmonic, Opera Idaho and the

American Festival Ballet (now Ballet Idaho), along with their respective youth-outreach programs: the Treasure Valley Youth Symphony, Ballet Idaho Academy of Dance and Opera Idaho's Children's Chorus.

The Simplot Academy opened in October 1992, culminating a six-year search by Esther Simplot for a space that could be the permanent home for the symphony, opera and ballet. With the whole-hearted support of her husband, Jack (the wealthiest man in Idaho; *figure* 126), Esther bought a former furniture warehouse for the modest sum of $50,000, spent $1.2 million in renovating it, and established a permanent endowment for its maintenance. The Simplots welcomed contributions from a large number of well-wishers, numbering 520 by the time the Academy opened, but it was and continues to be heavily dependent on the Simplot family for its financial support. In subsequent years, the 33,000 square feet in the original building at the corner of Ninth and Myrtle were substantially increased with the acquisition of two neighboring buildings on Eighth Street. The spacious three-building campus houses offices for the three organizations, as well as rehearsal and performance spaces. Music lovers are treated to a wide variety of performances, ranging from concerts by the Langroise Trio, Master Chorale and ensembles drawn

Fig. 126: J.R. "Jack" and Esther Simplot, c. 1980s. (Schmitz)

from Philharmonic musicians. Far less visible to the general public but critically important to the long-term welfare of the symphony, opera, and ballet is the assurance that they have a secure home free from the burdens of finding funding to support it.

IDAHO CENTER

While granting the importance of the Simplot Academy, nothing could match the massive impact on the geographic configuration of concerts in the Boise metropolitan area of the Idaho Center, opening in May 1997 on the northeast edge of Nampa. As Michael Deeds, popular music critic for the *Statesman*, put it rather belatedly a year later, following the Eric Clapton show, "move over Boise, the Treasure Valley's new hot spot for major concerts is Nampa." Boiseans were slow to accept this change. The *Statesman* devoted most of its coverage of the May 25 opening concert by the Moody Blues, accompanied by the Boise Philharmonic, to the traffic jams and paucity of parking that hampered those trying to attend. The Idaho Center management quickly set to work improving highway access and the supply of parking and forced Boiseans to take heed of this new venue by booking major entertainers, such as Barry Manilow on June 13.

Ironically enough, music concerts played a distinctly secondary role in the planning for the Idaho Center. Its primary purpose was to provide a new home for the Snake River Stampede, the most noted rodeo in southern Idaho, while supporting the urban renewal of northeast Nampa. As late as April 1998, Center director Rod Orrison declared, "first and foremost this is an agricultural center." Nevertheless, by the spring of 1998 the Idaho Center management had recognized its importance for the area's popular music concerts (*figure* 127). It sagely invested $300,000 to add a 2 ½ acre outdoor amphitheater that could seat 10,000 to 13,000 people listening to

rock bands playing as loud as they wished, since there were few residents within earshot. With another 13,000 seats indoors, the Idaho Center had a clear competitive advantage over all other concert venues in the area, as evidenced by a crowd numbering 25,000 at the August 1999 Neil Diamond concert.

The opening of the Idaho Center raised a question in the minds of many pop and rock music enthusiasts: Was there a sufficient market in the Boise area to support all of the major venues?

"It's as if," as the Pavilion's events manager phrased it, "someone built a new ski resort right next to Bogus Basin." Actually, it was even worse. With the September 1997 opening of the Bank of America Centre in downtown Boise, the area's seating capacity had more than doubled in just three months. The B of A Centre, a sports arena adjoining the Grove Hotel on Front Street, could seat 5,000 for a concert—not enough to seriously threaten the BSU Pavilion or Idaho Center, but still able to lure

Fig. 127: Idaho Center, Rock & Worship Roadshow, 2009. (farm4.static.flickr.com)

away a profitable mid-sized attraction. An Allman Brothers concert the week following the opening of the B of A Centre drew an audience of 3,300. This "first true test of rock concert stamina," according to Michael Deeds, yielded a "festive but not quite remarkable evening."

The answer to the question turned out to be a qualified yes. Both the Pavilion and Idaho Center enjoyed strong institutional and vital financial support— BSU for the Pavilion, the Harvest Festival (the organization that stages the annual Snake River Stampede) and the Nampa urban renewal program for the Idaho Center. In addition, these venues reached out to gain new attractions. Beginning in December 1997, the Boston Pops touring orchestra presented a Christmas concert at the Pavilion. The Idaho Center amphitheater drew the annual Warped Tour, a rock festival featuring numerous bands and an audience sporting weird haircuts and eccentric dress. So the two largest venues managed to survive, though without the comfortably large returns enjoyed by the Pavilion in its first years. The Bank of America Centre, on the other hand, barely managed to sustain a limited concert program and

clearly remained an "also ran" in the competition for major attractions.

SWAYNE AUDITORIUM

Six months after the opening of the Idaho Center in 1997, Nampa got its third new concert hall, rounding out its options for music performances. Northwest Nazarene College's Swayne Auditorium, seating 1,500, provided for concerts midway in audience size between the relatively intimate Civic Center and the vast Idaho Center. The Boise Philharmonic moved its Nampa concerts from the Civic Center to Swayne Auditorium soon after it opened, but generally the new hall posed no competitive challenges to existing concert venues. Rather, it provided a significant enhancement to the music life of the area with a concert schedule reflecting the conservative religious

character of the college.

Swayne Auditorium is housed in the Brandt Fine Arts Center (*figure* 128), a facility costing $5.2 million named for Samuel Swayne, a local doctor whose family contributed $1 million for the Auditorium. Its external appearance marked something of a departure

Fig. 128: Swayne Auditorium, Brandt Fine Arts Center, Northwest Nazarene University, Nampa, c. 2000. (Internet)

from the Spartan simplicity of most of the campus buildings, and the music programming for the Auditorium also reflected a comparable new, more ambitious music life for the college. For most of its existence, the college (which became Northwest Nazarene University in 1999) played only a very modest role in the area's concert life. Other than performances by its outstanding choirs, particularly the Northwesterners, and an annual presentation of Handel's "Messiah," the college offered few attractions for area music lovers. That began to change in the years just prior to the opening of Swayne Auditorium; students staged "Hello, Dolly!" in May 1995. Nevertheless, the opening of the Auditorium in November 1997

Music" in March 2000. But that religious commitment was broadened beyond its traditional evangelistic base to include artistically ambitious works such as John Rutter's "Requiem" in March 1998, Mendelssohn's "Elijah" in March 2001, and Fauré's "Requiem" in February 2000. In addition, there were hearty servings of secular music, ranging from

PROLIFERATING PERFORMING GROUPS

Up to this point in this chapter we have focused on structures, but the metro-wide diversification of music so characteristic of the 1990s went well beyond the construction of concert halls. There were also many new performing groups, reversing the trend of the 1970s when it appeared that performing groups in the Boise area were shrinking in number as they grew in professional quality. For example, the Meridian Community Orchestra organized in late 1990 and gradually grew to include about 70 musicians from across the metro area in what eventually became known as the Meridian Symphony. It performed in various suburban school auditoria, most commonly at Meridian Middle School, with a repertoire emphasizing "pieces that have a familiar feel." Richard Roller, the conductor, readily conceded, "I'd put us a distinct second behind the Boise Philharmonic, but we are actually getting better." In contrast to this unembarrassed amateurism, the Boise Baroque Orchestra, founded by Roller in 2003, stressed that it was made

Fig. 129: Boise Baroque Orchestra, Jewett Auditorium, College of Idaho, 2003. (Internet)

marked a quantum leap in the character of concerts at the college. Not that its religious commitment was in any sense slighted. The Crusader Choir and Halleluyah Brass Concert Band had prominent places on the program for the opening concert. And there were frequent concerts of religious music, such as "An Evening of Gospel

NNU's Jazz Big Band to Broadway musicals, including "Fiddler on the Roof," "Phantom of the Opera" and "My Fair Lady." It's hard to say how many Boiseans partook of the Swayne Auditorium offerings, but there is no doubt that they provided a whole new concert scene for Nampans.

up of professional musicians, many of whom also played with the Philharmonic. Conducted by Daniel Stern since 2005, this small chamber orchestra specialized in the works of Bach and other early masters. Each of its concerts were given in Canyon County, either at Nampa Civic Center or Jewett Auditorium, as well as at the Cathedral of the Rockies in Boise (*figure* 129).

Fig. 130: Whitney Women's Chorale, c. 1990s, and fundraiser cookbook (Panko)

Choral groups also saw a rejuvenation in the last years of the 20th century. Frequently, they drew on a church background but went on to perform a wide range of secular as well as religious music. Thus the Whitney Women's Chorale (*figure* 130) , founded in 1982 and directed for many years by Constance Branton, was based at Whitney Methodist Church but also performed elsewhere in Boise. Even its concerts at its home church ranged widely in the music performed. For example, in November 1992 the Chorale presented "An Evening of Broadway Hits," including singers from the Boise Opera Chorus and BSU choirs. The group also toured annually, both nationally and even overseas. Reflecting its lighthearted refusal to take itself too seriously, it raised money for its tours by issuing a cookbook "from the Singing Potluck Professionals" (*figure* 130).

In another innovation, for the first time in Boise's history ethnic groups found not only a voice but a continuing audience. We have noted in earlier chapters the marginalization of the small black community in Boise. By the 1990s, however, gospel music could be heard in a wide variety of settings, including an annual workshop at BSU widely covered by the local media. St. Paul Baptist Church (probably the largest black congregation in Boise) felt comfortable having its choir offer a number of gospel music concerts. The Basque population far outnumbered the black, but although the Oinkari Dancers had long since gained a national reputation, only belatedly did the Basque community also develop a choral group. In 1986 Biotzetik, sponsored by the Basque Museum, began to give occasional concerts in the Boise area.

A Unique Synthesis

The 1990s brought many new developments to the Boise music. Perhaps the most remarkable reflected the culmination of Gene Harris's love affair with Idaho. Since moving to Boise in 1977, he had become convinced his new home was the ideal place to live. A lengthy profile published in the June 7, 1988, *Wall Street Journal* quoted him saying "If you haven't seen Idaho, you don't know what heaven is." Two years later, he assured the crowd at Ste. Chapelle "Idaho is a little

Fig. 131: Gene Harris Jazz Festival poster. (Internet)

piece of heaven." He responded to his adopted state not only in his musical performances but also by becoming one of Boise's most influential music patrons. In the process, he established a unique synthesis of art and public affairs.

Gene Harris' performances spanned a very wide range of settings. We have already seen that he initiated the open-air jazz concerts at Ste. Chapelle and launched Alive After Five. Here are three examples from the 1990s of his virtuosity, beginning with his schedule in March 1992. On the 7th, he and his trio performed as guest artists with the Boise Philharmonic at the Morrison Center. They opened with Harris's version of "Battle Hymn of the Republic" followed by five jazz pieces, including "Can't Help Loving that Man." The next day, he and the trio left on a three-month tour to Australia, Hong Kong and elsewhere in the Far East.

Fig. 132: Phil Batt, campaigning for governor, 1993. (Schmitz)

Second, on March 25, 1993, he presented "An Evening with Gene Harris and His Friends" as a benefit for Phil Batt's campaign for governor. It remained unclear whether this was an indication of Harris' political sympathies or his fondness for a friend who occasionally joined in Harris's jam sessions at the Idanha with his clarinet (*figure* 132). Third, as an expression of his religious faith, which he believed saved him from the loss of eyesight resulting from diabetes, he issued in 1997 a CD, "In His Hands," which a *Statesman* reviewer thought "feels like an intimate gospel service in your living room."

The variety and success of his concerts might well have been sufficient for any other musician, but Gene Harris wanted to do something really special for Boise, so he conceived of and initiated the Gene Harris Jazz Festival (*figure* 131). In September 1996, he announced his plans for the Festival. It would feature nationally known jazz musicians and also create opportunities for students to attend workshops and perform. The proceeds of the Festival would go to an endowment to provide scholarships for BSU music students. He kicked off the endowment fund drive with a concert on the 29th at the Morrison Center. Typical of Harris's style, tickets for the concert were free and the audience was requested to make contributions to the fund.

The first Festival ran from April 8 to 10, 1998, with Gene Harris, Steve Hampton and Marcus Printop on trumpet, a number of other headliners, and 1,000 students in the workshops. "Club Night" on the 8th was staged in several cabarets in the Eighth and Idaho to Capitol Boulevard area downtown. The guest artists were featured on the 9th, and the Festival ended on the 10th with Gene Harris at the Pavilion. Attendance was good at the first Festival and grew appreciably in subsequent years. It is too early to tell how significant the scholarship endowment fund will turn out to be, but the annual Festival continues to generate a mix of lively street life and huge concert audiences that might almost be seen as a 21st century equivalent of Music Week in its first years. Gene Harris lived to see only the first two of his festivals. His deteriorating health brought his life to an end in January 2000. Some of those mourning his passing must have feared that it ended what could have been the greatest musical inspiration in Boise's history.

A Continuing Legacy

Fig. 133: Curtis Stigers, jazz performance, c. 2003 (Internet)

A number of musicians were determined to keep Gene Harris' inspiration alive, however. Some did this by staging annual Gene Harris Memorial concerts at Boise and Ste. Chapelle. Others persuaded the City Council to name the Julia Davis Park bandshell in his honor. And others carried on Harris's musical tradition—particularly Curtis Stigers, whose international success as a jazzy blues singer (*figure* 133) and songwriter clearly reflects the influence of Gene Harris.

Although Stigers was born in Los Angeles in 1965, he moved to Boise at the age of 9 and graduated from Capital High School. During his teenage years, he and friends such as Paul Tillotson closely followed Harris's performances and sometimes sat in at his jam sessions. Harris refused to take on students, but Stigers made himself a Harris protegé, and Harris genially accepted his followers. By 1987, Stigers' band, the Young Jazz Lions, was playing DJ's, a local night club where Gene Harris also regularly appeared. Later that year, the band broke up, with several of the members going off to college. Stigers preferred to pursue his career by moving to New York City and striving to make it in the big time, but he never severed his ties with Boise. Each year he would come home to visit friends and family and play a few local gigs. Meanwhile, he quickly made a name for himself nationally as a pop singer. He was covered by *GQ* magazine in August 1988 and was a featured guest on The Tonight Show in November 1991. Clearly, by 1992 he had become a national star—"Hits the Big Time," as the *Boise Weekly* put it in announcing his two-night concert at the Morrison Center.

Through all of his growing national success, Stigers continued to stay close to Gene Harris. At the first Gene Harris Festival, Stigers joined Harris in the Pavilion concert. And following Harris's death, Stigers carried on the tradition by playing at Ste. Chapelle. Most important, he followed Harris's example of keeping his roots in Boise even while performing throughout North America and across Europe. Rosalie Sorrels has said she delayed moving back to Boise so long because she couldn't make a living here.

Fig. 135: "Faust" poster, Opera Idaho, 2009. (Internet)

Harris in the 1980s had shown that in the jet age a successful musician need not live where he worked; he could enjoy living in Boise and tour internationally. Stigers followed that example by leaving New York in 2003 and moving back home to Boise. Whatever residual fear might be lingering that Boise was somehow too remote to be connected fully to the national scene was conclusively refuted by Gene Harris, followed by Curtis Stigers.

AND THE MUSIC PLAYS ON

Boise's concert life during the first decade of the 21st century continued without significant disruptions or troubling changes. As I write this, the latest issue of the *Statesman*'s weekly entertainment guide ("Scene," Dec. 4, 2011) offers attractions much like those in an issue of a decade earlier. The highlights for the weekend include Opera Idaho's presentation of "Amahl and the Night Visitors" at the Egyptian Theater and BSU music department's annual "Family Holiday Concert" at the Morrison Center, with ticket prices very modestly set at $8 for adults and only $1 for children. Forthcoming shows at the Morrison Center include "My Fair Lady" on January 3-5 and "Damn Yankees" on March 13-15.

The continuity evident in those offerings can also be seen in other aspects of the local music scene. The schools still produce a large number of talented musicians, some of whom march in the bands playing in local parades, others performing in widely recognized groups such as the Boise High chamber

Fig. 134: St. Michael's Episcopal Cathedral, 2006. (Neil)

orchestra, which accepted an invitation to an international festival in Banff, Canada, and in 2000 another in Vienna, Austria. The churches that had long and distinguished records in music kept up the pace. St. Michael's Cathedral, for example, presented Vivaldi's "Gloria" in 2006 (*figure* 134), and the Cathedral of the Rockies' very popular "Christmas at the Cathedral" was offered in 2011 as it had been for the previous 50 years.

Changes did occur, of course. For the Philharmonic, there was a change in leadership when James Ogle retired at the end of the 2007 season. This was handled adeptly by having each of the finalists in the competition to succeed Ogle conduct a concert during the 2007/8 season. The final selection of Robert Franz, associate conductor of the Houston symphony, received widespread acclamation from both the musicians and the audiences. For the Master Chorale, change came in 2011 when it freed itself from the burdens of management by merging with the Philharmonic.

Boise's ability to absorb change while maintaining continuity could be illustrated by a wide variety of instances, but one particularly telling example would be the production of Charles Gounod's opera, "Faust." It has been performed in Boise on several occasions, the first time in 1922 for Music Week and most recently in October 2009 by Opera Idaho (*figure* 135). Both then and now, the highly moralistic story was presented with a large combination of singers, dancers, and instrumentalists. But the presentations greatly differed when it came to the staging of the opera. In 1922, it was presented "in concert form"—that is, more of a choral cantata than a theater production (although it did include live dancers). The lead singers wore dress clothes rather than costumes and several *tableaux vivants* replaced stage action. The 2009 performance, on the other hand, included costumes, stage sets and all of the sights as well as the sounds one expects of an

opera production. Equally important were the specific venues. In 1922, it was outdoors, free of charge, and drew an audience numbering several thousand. In 2009, it was in the new South Junior High School Auditorium, seating 900, with no expectation that most Boiseans

Fig. 136: Boise Music Festival, Ann Morrison Park, 2011. (Internet)

might attend. Opera continues to play an important part in Boise's music life, and Opera Idaho, assisted by the Boise Philharmonic, surely evinces a greater professionalism than could the Civic Festival Chorus in 1922, but it now caters to a far more limited portion of the public.

Popular music, successful in reaching out to a much larger portion of the public, also continued to thrive in the new century. An attractive new amphitheater, the Eagle River Pavilion, opened on June 10, 2010, with Crosby, Stills and Nash

providing the premier performance. While a good deal smaller than Idaho Center's amphitheater, the Eagle River Pavilion has a far more scenic setting, along the banks of the Boise River. Back in the city of Boise, there lingered a desire for something to fill the gap left when the Boise River Festival ended. That was met in July 2010, when Peak Broadcasting, which operates several local radio stations, sponsored the first Boise Music Festival in Ann Morrison Park. A day-long affair with numerous bands and free to the public, it drew an audience numbering tens of thousands. On July 23, 2011, the Festival counted over 70,000 in attendance (*figure* 136).

It's obviously quite a distance in time and setting from the Columbia Band playing at Ninth and Main to a variety of rock bands playing in Ann Morrison Park. Yet the Boise Music Festival can be seen as recognizably following the tradition set back in 1910 by the Columbia Band—a tradition of reaching out to all of the people in Boise with music that is freely accessible and enjoyable for most, if not all, of those who hear it. Boise Pops is surely alive and well, with a great future to be realized as time goes on.

Index